Patterns

of Race

in the Americas

Patterns
of Race
in the Americas

Marvin Harris

Columbia University

The Norton Library
W·W·NORTON & COMPANY·INC·
NEW YORK

COPYRIGHT © 1964 BY WALKER AND COMPANY, A DIVISION
OF PUBLICATIONS DEVELOPMENT CORPORATION

First published in the Norton Library 1974
by arrangement with Walker and Company

Books That Live
The Norton imprint on a book means that in the publisher's
estimation it is a book not for a single season but for the years.
W. W. Norton & Company, Inc.

Library of Congress Cataloging in Publication Data
Harris, Marvin, 1927–
    Patterns of race in the Americas.
    (The Norton library)
    Reprint of the ed. published by Walker, New York,
which was issued as no. 1 of the Walker summit library.
    Bibliography: p.
    1. Latin America—Race question. 2. Ethnology—
Latin America. I. Title.
[F1419.A1H3   1974]   301.45'1'042098   74-803
ISBN 0-393-00727-8

Printed in the United States of America
1 2 3 4 5 6 7 8 9 0

TABLE OF CONTENTS

Part I: Interpretation

Part II: Reference

v

1 / Before Columbus

The peoples and cultures of all of the American nations are to some extent hybrid products of centuries of racial and cultural mixture. This is especially true of Latin America, which much more aptly than the United States may be described as a melting pot. Genetically, the population of Latin America consists in about equal measure of contributions from Caucasoid, Negroid and Amerindian types, while in the United States both the Indians and Negroes together do not amount to more than 10 per cent of the population. Moreover, although European cultural elements are dominant in both regions, the contributions of African and American Indian cultures to Latin America are more widespread and significant than is true of the United States.

Despite the profusion of racial and cultural types in Latin America, a rather simple pattern or grand design can be discerned. The contribution of the American Indian, racially and culturally speaking, is greatest in the highland backbone of Mesoamerica and the Central Andes of South America. All the way from Mexico through the Central American republics, branching off into highland Venezuela and then south again through Colombia, Ecuador, Peru and northern Chile, the highlands display a considerable amount of cultural and physical hybridization between European and American Indian traits. On the other hand, in the lowland coastal portions of Latin America, including the islands of the Caribbean and the eastern littoral of South America within the confines of the tropical and semi-tropical latitudes, African and European cultural and racial mixtures predominate. Actually, wherever there are tropical coastal lowlands, whether on the east or west coasts of Central and South America, there one finds conspicuous admixtures of African genetic and cultural influences. Finally, to complete the picture, the non-tropical portions of the Latin American lowlands, including southern Brazil, Uruguay, central Chile and northern Argentina, are inhabited by the greatest concentration of Europeans unaffected by conspicuous American Indian or Negro, cultural or racial influences.

For Latin America, therefore, the major anthropo-geographical equation reads: Highlands: American Indians, Europeans and their mixtures. Tropical and semi-tropical coastal lowlands: Africans, Europeans and their mixtures. Temperate south: Europeans.[1]

What accounts for this distribution of racial and cultural ingredients in the Latin American melting pot? Since the Negro influence is greatest in the tropical and semi-tropical lowlands, and since this pattern is repeated in the United States, one is tempted to conclude that climate is the predominant factor. This conclusion receives further support from the fact that the densest concentrations of Europeans without significant Indian and Negro admixtures are to be found in the temperate lowland regions in North as well as South America. But although climate does play a role in explaining the distribution of the racial and cultural stocks of the New World, it is by no means the only or even the most significant factor to be considered.

That this is so should be obvious enough from the fact that the American Indians in pre-contact times inhabited not only the highlands but the entire New World. The replacement of American Indians by Africans in the coastal lowlands, therefore, cannot be simply a matter of climate, for the aboriginal populations of the New World were obviously perfectly capable of maintaining their existence under tropical and semi-tropical conditions.

In order to understand the present-day distribution of racial and cultural types in the New World, the variable which initially deserves emphasis is the nature of the aboriginal societies with which the Europeans came into contact. One of the most important features of the American environment from the point of view of the European colonists, whether *conquistadores* or pilgrims, was not the climate or the topography. It was instead the level of sociocultural integration characteristic of the Amerindian societies with which the Europeans were obliged to interact.[2]

During the 25,000 years or so which preceded the coming of the Europeans, the American Indians had evolved along numerous divergent lines. Cultures had developed which were adapted to sea coast, forest, plains, riverine, arctic and many other specific kinds of environments. But in addition to this specific kind of evolutionary growth there took place an over-all or general development whose principal stages were remarkably parallel to those which had unfolded in the Old World.[3] At the time the Europeans arrived on the scene large portions of the New World had come under the influence of centralized native states. Other areas were occupied by American Indians living on a tribal or village level of social organization. Others were yet more primitive. None of the state-level societies had originated or spread north of Mexico.

The advanced Indian societies consisted of densely settled agriculturists. These peoples were organized into class-structured groups, some of which had begun to develop cities and powerful and elaborate theocratic and political bureaucracies. In architecture, metallurgy, astronomy and statecraft, the most highly developed of the native American states were fully comparable with the kind of Old World civilizations which had evolved independently somewhat earlier in Egypt, Mesopotamia and the Indus Valley.

By and large, these aboriginal American Indian native states and incipient empires, with their elaborate class structures, their monumental architecture and their bureaucratic centers, were located in what I have previously defined as the highland portions of Latin America.[4]

In contrast, the rest of the New World, including lowland Latin America, was inhabited by aboriginal groups which lacked social stratification, state bureaucracies, cities and monumental architecture. Although many of the pre-state peoples gained their livelihood primarily from agriculture, the methods involved were markedly different from those characteristic of the highland regions. Lowland agriculture depended to a large extent upon the labor of women in its planting, weeding and harvesting phases. Men contributed to the agricultural production of the lowland peoples primarily by clearing and burning the underbrush in conformity with the process known as "slash-and-burn," "shifting" or "fire" agriculture. During the rest of the year a considerable amount of their time was devoted to hunting and fishing.

Although slash-and-burn techniques, under certain rare and up to now unexplained circumstances, have been made to yield agricultural surpluses sufficient to support civilizations, for the most part this mode of agricultural production destines the populations employing it to remain relatively sparse.[5] The controlling factor is probably the availability of forest, for as the underbrush is cut, dried and set afire, the vegetation upon which the entire cycle depends is consumed. At the end of a period of anywhere from ten to twenty years, the village is forced to move to another location where secondary growth permits the renewal of the cycle. The need for large areas of secondary growth, with the consequent high probability if not inevitability of a semi-migratory type of existence, has a drastic limiting influence on population density. As a further consequence, it also exerts a limiting influence on the nature of the social organization which can be supported by the slash-and-burn agricultural base. Low agricultural yields and low densities of population did not permit the formation of native elites, of classes with special power prerogatives expressed in differential access to strategic resources, or the development of priesthoods with their specialized astronomical learning, craft specialists and most of the other forms of urban or non-agricultural specializations.[6] Instead, the lowland peoples, prior to European contact, were predominantly organized on an egalitarian basis. Chieftainship occurred to some extent, but the power of the chief rested primarily upon persuasion rather than upon ability to command specialists in the maintenance of law and order or upon the

4

ability to deprive others of access to those portions of the environment necessary for the maintenance of life. In this regard the lowland Latin American tribes resembled the eastern woodland Indians of the United States, such as the Iroquois and the Mohicans. Indeed, such Brazilian lowland groups as the Tupinambá and the Guarani were essentially similar to their northern woodland counterparts in many respects. Their villages, for example, were made up of long houses, in which resided the members of clan-related lineages. They placed great stress upon hunting ability and upon physical endurance for both men and women, and they emphasized bravery in warfare above all else as the supreme male virtue. Although the tropical lowland peoples took prisoners of war and brought them back to their own villages, they did not systematically make use of the labor of these captives. Apparently, slash-and-burn agriculture was not capable of sustaining a village population augmented by the incorporation of a slave caste. Instead, prisoners of war were fattened up for a while and then at a critical point in the tribe's ceremonial cycle, the prisoner would be handed a club and tied to a post at the center of the village. There he defended himself as best he could against his executioners, male and female, who seized the opportunity to get rid of their deepest frustrations.[7]

The highland American Indian civilizations were separated from the lowland Indian tribes by a gulf at least as great as that which separated Caesar's Rome from the barbarian areas of Europe. The most tangible evidence of this great contrast is to be found in the numerous and impressive architectural accomplishments of the pre-Columbian inhabitants of Mexico, Guatemala, Ecuador, Peru and Bolivia. In Mexico and Central America great pyramids, elaborately carved statuary, colonnaded temples and palaces, and ruins of cities which had once spread over hundreds of acres impress even the casual visitor with their monumental scope. Some of these ruins date back to the very beginning of the Christian era. What was probably the largest aboriginal city in the New World, Teotihuacan, situated a few miles north of Mexico City, had reached its maximum development as long ago as A.D. 800. The ruins of this city are scattered over an area of some 2,000 acres and feature a complex of avenues, temples, courts and pyramids of heroic dimensions.

At Teotihuacan there is the Pyramid of the Sun, 1,300,000 cubic yards of adobe bricks faced with stone and plaster. This pyramid measures 689 by 689 feet at the base and rises to a height of 210 feet. At Cholula in the state of Puebla, Mexico, there is another artificial mountain, dating from about the same period, which in terms of cubic content is larger than the Pyramid of Cheops and which is still one of the largest single edifices ever constructed.

Modern Mexico City itself is built on the ruins of Tenochtitlan, the ancient capital of the Aztecs. Tenochtitlan occupied an island in Lake Texcoco, was connected to the mainland by artificial causeways, and contained a large network of canals and bridges. Its population at the time of conquest may have been as high as 300,000 people.[8]

In South America evidence of pre-Columbian architectural achievement is no less spectacular. Vast engineering projects were carried out as early as A.D. 500 to bring water to Peru's coastal valleys. At Chicama there is an earth-filled aqueduct which bridges a ravine a mile wide at a height of 50 feet. It is estimated that over a million cubic yards of fill were employed in its construction.

Near the modern city of Trujillo is found the largest of the South American pre-Columbian structures, the Temple of the Sun. This is a pyramid built on a platform 60 feet high and 750 feet long by 450 in width. The pyramid rises to a height of 75 feet and the entire structure was constructed out of approximately 130 million adobe bricks.

In the Andean Highlands megalithic masonry construction takes the place of adobe. At Tiahuanaco, near Bolivia's Lake Titicaca, megalithic archways and statues have been discovered. From a later period there is the astonishing fortress of Sacsahuaman located near Cuzco, the ancient capital of the Inca Empire. Here vast megaliths, weighing up to 300 tons apiece, were fitted together with microscopic precision to form 30-foot-high walls. Equally impressive is the network of roads constructed during Inca times. Many of these ran in straight lines with uniform width across obstacles, and over difficult terrain. Suspension bridges, measuring up to 200 feet in length, were built across ravines and rivers.

No less spectacular than the monumental architectural achievements are the crafts and artistic specialties of the pre-Columbian state-level civilizations. In pre-Columbian Peru ceramic craft and textile manufacture reached heights of excellence fully comparable to those of the best potters and weavers of Europe. Independently of the Old World, New World Indian artisans discovered for themselves metallurgical techniques appropriate for bronze, silver and gold. They had not, however, come to the point of mass-producing metallurgical objects nor had they begun to develop a repertory of metal tools, but this deficiency renders the monumental stoneworking achievements all the more remarkable.

As a further testimony to the contrast between the pre-Columbian civilizations and the egalitarian American Indian tribes, the development in Mesoamerica of writing and of a calendar more accurate than that employed in contemporary Europe should also be mentioned. And in one achievement at least, the American civilizations had proceeded further than their counterparts in Europe. Long before the concept of the zero had become part of European mathematics, the ancient Maya were regularly using a zero glyph in their extremely accurate calculations of astronomical events.

The agriculture of the pre-Columbian American Indian, civilizations was also fully equivalent to that of Europe at a comparable point of development. In Peru great networks of inter-valley aqueducts and canals were responsible for maintaining the specialization and bureaucratic elaboration of the ancient states. Under the Inca whole mountainsides were graded and terraced into luxuriant gardens. In Mesoamerica, especially in the Valley of Mexico, equally intensive forms of agriculture were practiced, based on permanent and flood-water irrigation, terracing, fertilization and permanent field rotation. The most productive method was that of *chinampas*, an intricate network of dredged-up fields, canals and ditches built up along the margins of Lake Texcoco.

The repertory of basic crops which powered the New

World civilizations was also in a very real sense at least equal if not superior to that of the Old World. Maize, the basic staple throughout much of aboriginal America, quickly became one of the most important food resources of Europe, Africa and Asia. Similarly the potato, a New World crop first domesticated in highland South America, spread around the world and modified the destinies of nations. Dozens of other important plants were also included in the American agricultural inventory, among which manioc, peanuts, beans, lima beans, tomatoes, avocadoes and sweet potatoes have since become most familiar to the rest of the world.

The real significance, however, of the aboriginal highland accomplishments in architecture, crafts, learning and agriculture lies in the testimony they render about the social organization of the societies which made use of them. These accomplishments imply the existence of two features generally absent in the lowland areas: specialization, and the organization and control of mass labor. Eric Wolf has estimated, for example, that in order to construct the Pyramid of the Sun at Teotihuacan, 10,000 men had labored over a period of ten years.[10] Probably as many as 30,000 men were employed at one time in the construction of the Inca's Sacsahuaman fortress.[11] Food, shelter and clothing had to be supplied to this army of workers, and similar problems of production, transport and distribution had to be solved in all of the monumental undertakings of the ancient New World civilizations.

The recruitment, maintenance and coordination and direction of this mass of laborers and specialists were vested in a bureaucratic, noble class: a small group of priests and rulers who exercised despotic control over the rank and file of peasants and artisans. Of the utmost significance for an understanding of contemporary Latin America is the existence of various forms of labor conscription, tribute and taxation in the New World aboriginal civilizations. By such methods the ancient despotic rulers were able to recruit the manpower and to gather the materials needed for state enterprises. Typically, the power holders in this system were so exalted above the common man that they were believed to be either the agents or the direct descendants of gods. The rank and file of the highland Indian population labored not only for themselves but on behalf of these god-priest rulers. The latter in turn repaid the efforts of the commoners by concentrating the surplus products of their intensive agriculture on the creation of monuments and works of a sacred nature deemed essential for the prosperity of the kingdom and for the continuity of the universe.

The most successful and perfectly coordinated of the Indian political systems was centered in Peru. From Cuzco, the ancient capital of the Inca Empire, the supreme Inca, considered to be a child of the sun, ruled a land extending for almost 2,000 miles north and south along the Andean Cordillera. The lives of perhaps as many as 6 million people were under the dominion of the Inca and his supporting bureaucracy.[12] Possibly as much as two-thirds of the work effort of the peasant masses was devoted to the production of food harvests which came under the control of the Inca and his agents. This production was regularly siphoned off by means of a system of national granaries to support state-sponsored construction of monuments, roads and temples. In addition, regular corvées, known as *mit'a,* were drawn from the local population and shifted about to the site of construction as needed. The Inca systematically recruited artisans into the special temple work force and they called up drafts of men to serve in the system of human pony express by which messages were speeded to all parts of the empire. They recruited, in addition, thousands to work in the royal mines, and to tend the herds of royal alpaca· and llama. Other thousands were destined for service in the armed forces. As a political follow-up to the conquest of new territories, the Inca moved entire populations from one area of the empire to another. These colonists, known as *mitimaes,* were part of the Inca plan to create homogeneous linguistic and ethnic groups throughout their domain.

It is interesting to note that the Inca Empire extended primarily north and south along a relatively narrow band, largely confined to the Andean Cordillera and the arid coastal plain. Although the Inca armies made forays down into the lowland tropical forest areas of the Amazon Basin, they never succeeded in extending their political control east of the Andes. They were unsuccessful for reasons closely

9

related to those which, as we shall see, also explain the failure of the Europeans to make significant use of the aboriginal populations living in the lowland areas for labor purposes. The Inca found that the tropical forest populations in the Amazon Basin were unconquerable. Living in scattered villages, they were able to withstand the full might of the Inca armies simply by melting away deeper into the forests, abandoning their small gardens and their few worldly possessions. There were no granaries to be seized, and few prisoners to be taken. Apparently, the Inca were successful in the expansion of their empire only when they came across developed state-organized societies which possessed fully sedentary villages, permanent fields and a dense population.

To a large extent, the basic patterns of race relations in the post-Columbian period emanate from the contrast between the highland and the lowland aboriginal cultures which I have just described. The differential results of contact between the European invaders and the state-organized pre-state groups flowed from the contrasting opportunities these groups offered for profit and power. These opportunities, as we shall see in the next chapter, were in turn essentially a question of the quantity, tractability and durability of the native labor supply.

2 / Race, Culture and Manpower

The kinds of accommodation which have been achieved by the various racial and cultural components in Latin America are in large measure the consequence of the attempt to harness the aboriginal population on behalf of European profit-making enterprises. It is true, of course, that the New World was richly endowed by nature with fertile soils, a great spectrum of climates, and enormous reserves of precious metals. These resources, however, were in themselves worthless. In order to farm the soil, there must be farmers, and in order to mine the earth, there must be miners. Without adequate manpower, even the fabulous mines of Potosí, still producing after 500 years of intensive operation, would have served no useful purpose.[1] Lesley Simpson's observation that "the Conquest of Mexico was the capture of native labor" applies no less aptly to all of Latin America.[2]

The problem of manpower in Latin America has been resolved in several radically different ways, each of which ultimately depends upon the nature of the pre-contact cultures and each of which in turn is associated in modern times with a particular pattern of race relations.

In the lowland areas the initial labor prospectus was poor indeed. The sparse aboriginal populations, semi-migratory in nature, were almost completely unaccustomed to intensive field labor, or corvée services. Just as the Inca had failed to dominate the tropical lowland peoples lying to the east of their empire, Europeans found it impossible to put the lowland Indians to work, except under a system of direct slavery. Enslavement of the lowland Amerindian groups, however, did not prove economically viable for reasons which I shall shortly recount.

The failure of the labor regime based upon the enslavement of lowland Indian groups led to the introduction into the New World of large numbers of laborers from Africa. These African contingents were localized in the tropical and semi-tropical lowlands of both North and South America and put to work on the production of plantation crops having high export value in the European markets. Meanwhile, a totally different potential for labor use was encountered in the highlands. There, once the native rulers had been removed or converted to puppets, the mass of commoners could with relative ease be put to work producing agricultural, industrial and mineral products for the benefit of the invaders. As a result, the contemporary population of the highland portions of Latin America exhibits only minute traces of Negro racial and African cultural mixtures. Let us now examine in some detail how this came about.

At the beginning of the conquest of the New World, the Spanish were optimistic about the potentialities of the lowland Indians for slave labor. Columbus himself had argued the feasibility of the enslavement of the Caribbean peoples and had envisaged a thriving slave trade between America and Europe. Enslavement of the Amerindians was easily justified on the grounds that they were not only heathens but cannibals. It was believed that many tribes could not be introduced to the virtues of Christianity or be made to work unless they were firmly controlled by their conquerors under the slave system.

Slaving expeditions ranged throughout the Caribbean Islands and along the coasts of Mexico and North and South America during the last years of the fifteenth century and the first decades of the sixteenth. It quickly became apparent, however, that Indian slavery was a doomed institution. Expeditions had to range further and further as the originally sparse population was decimated by the raiding, by disease, and by excessive toil. Indian slaves died by the thousands while engaged in labor on behalf of their conquerors. Many committed suicide; others disappeared into the forests never to be seen again. Especially devastating was their lack of immunity against European diseases such as measles, smallpox and respiratory infections. By the end of the seventeenth century, practically the entire Indian population of the Caribbean had been wiped out.[3] A similar situation prevailed in Brazil. The males no less than the females of the Brazilian coastal tribes turned out to be very poor field hands and their high rate of mortality made them very poor investments. "The expenditure of human life here in Bahia these past twenty years," said one Jesuit father in 1583, "is a thing that is hard to believe; for no one could believe that so great a supply could ever be exhausted, much less in so short a time."[4]

As the supply of lowland Indian slaves diminished, the Portuguese and lowland Spanish colonists looked to Africa for their labor force. This turn of events, which was to have such long-lasting consequences for the entire world, was not due to any sudden realization that Africa contained a greater manpower pool than the American lowlands. Long before the transatlantic trade began, both the Spanish and Portuguese were well aware that Africa could be made to yield up its human treasure. But in the early part of the sixteenth century the cost of transporting large numbers of slaves across the Atlantic was excessive in relation to the profits which could be extracted from their labor. This situation changed radically when, toward the middle of the century (somewhat later in the Dutch and English Caribbean possessions), sugar cane plantings were begun in Brazil. With the introduction of chocolate (a New World crop) and the spread of the coffee-drinking habit in Europe, the world consumption of sugar had suddenly skyrocketed, and by the end of the sixteenth century sugar had become the most valuable agricultural commodity in international trade. The importation of Negroes from Africa now became economically feasible. Although the costs of transporting Africans across the Atlantic Ocean remained high, the profits which could be wrung from their labor on the sugar estates were still higher. It was thus that the craving of Europe for sweets and coffee wiped out the aboriginal population of a large portion of the New World and condemned millions from another continent to a short and toilsome life.

In seeking for an explanation of why the lowland sugar planters regarded one Negro slave as the equivalent of five Indians, one must guard against interpretations based upon biological factors.[5] It is frequently asserted, for example, that the greater adaptability of the Negro to slavery conditions on the tropical lowland plantations was a result of his ability to withstand the intense heat and humidity of the tropics. There is no reason, however, to conclude that the Indians were biologically any less adapted to life in the tropics than the Negroes were. Nor is there any reason whatsoever to conclude that the Negroes were by nature any more servile than the Indians. In the highland regions, where the culture was different, the Indians were also reduced to servility, and their semi-slave condition has endured into the present century.

There are two other factors which better explain the preference expressed by the lowland planters for Negro rather than for Indian field hands. One is that the Africans had been pre-adapted by their cultural experience to cope with the demands of regular field labor. It is well known that slavery, serfdom and corvée were on-going institutions in many sub-Saharan African societies before European contact. To be sure, the scope and intensity of slavery under African aboriginal conditions were not comparable to the system which developed after the Europeans began to promote slavery and slave-raiding on a massive scale in order to satisfy the labor requirements of the New World. But groups such as those of Yoruba, Dahomey, Ashanti, Ife, Oyo and Congo, from which the bulk of the slaves was probably brought, were societies in which considerable differences in rank existed.[6] Moreover, throughout much of Negro Africa, males made a more important contribution to agriculture than was true among the typical Amerindian lowland tribes.

The second relevant point is that the Negroes, over centuries of indirect contact with North Africa and Europe, probably had acquired immunities to certain common European disease organisms which were lethal to the American Indians. Epidemics of catastrophic proportions kept recurring all through the first centuries of contact between the Europeans and Indians. A third of the population of the Tupinambá in the vicinity of Bahia, for example, was wiped out by smallpox in 1562, and to judge from the modern experience of the Brazilian Service for the Protection of Indians, measles and the common cold were probably just as devastating.[7] Recent demographic studies of central Mexico during the sixteenth century reveal that an astonishing decline in population occurred after contact. Borah and Cook claim that the people of Central Mexico were reduced in numbers from something close to 20 million to about 1 million in less than one hundred years.[8] It is clear that this decline must be attributed in no small part to the interplay between the new diseases and the general disruption introduced by the invaders.

Also relevant here is the puzzling solicitude which many of the Spanish labor laws display on behalf of the Indians.[9] The labor code of 1609, for example, prohibited the employment of Indians at certain tasks connected with sugar processing because of their alleged lack of physical stamina. Indeed, the Spanish and Portuguese generally were of the opinion that the Indians were by nature weaker than the Negroes. But this can only mean (in view of the fantastic feats of stamina characteristic of healthy Amerindian carriers and laborers) that the Indians more readily fell victims to European pathogens. A third factor might also be found in the tremendous incidence of mortality among the Negro slaves during their passage to the New World. The selective effect of this terrifying journey (following upon forced marches to the African slave entrepôts) must have meant that only remarkably resistant individuals survived. Furthermore, as suggested by Gonzalo Beltrán for Mexico, Africans tended to be selected for youth and vitality much more systematically than was possible in the case of Indians.[10] Thus, although African slaves cost five to ten times more than Indian slaves, they were a safer investment. Whatever the reasons for the preference for Negroes by the lowland planters, it is clear that the demography of the New World would ultimately have left them no choice in the matter. Despite their alleged physical inferiority, Indians were employed as slaves on the Brazilian plantations and they continued to be hunted until in effect there were none left except in the most remote parts of the jungle.

At the very time when the African slave trade was beginning to develop into one of the world's most important commercial ventures, the Spanish Crown passed laws prohibiting the enslavement of Indians in its New World possessions. (During the period 1580-1640, when Portugal and Spain were ruled by the same monarchs, these laws also applied to Brazil.) A great deal of romantic nonsense pervades the attempts to explain this paradox. The Spanish Crown is pictured as being influenced by the crusading religious missionary Bartolomé de Las Casas to abandon the policy of Indian slavery in its New World possessions out of humanitarian and religious convictions. There is no doubt that men like Las Casas, Fray García de Loaisa, and Francisco de Vitoria, who were primarily responsible for the promulgation of the famous New Laws of 1542,[11] were motivated by sincere and deep humanitarian convictions. There is no doubt also that the Spanish Crown was sensitive to moral and religious arguments. However, neither the special pleadings of the clerics nor the sensibilities of the monarchs lacked roots in material interests. The mission of the Church was to save souls. The power of the Church was directly related to the number of converts and hence if for no other reason the Church could not stand idly by while the aboriginal population of the New World was destroyed by the colonists. Furthermore, it was not against slavery in general that the Church fought but rather specifically against the enslavement of Indians by the colonists. On the issue of African slavery, the Spanish Church very early adopted an essentially hands-off position. Few churchmen expressed any moral reservations about the slave trade with Africa. On the contrary, the enslavement of Negroes was frequently viewed as a religious duty consonant with the highest moral principles.[12] This was equally true of the Church in Brazil, where "the Portuguese Jesuits too often demonstrated that they would permit slavery provided they could control it. They owned Indian as well as Negro slaves."[13]

The most plausible explanation of the New Laws is that they represented the intersection of the interests of three power groups: the Church, the Crown and the colonists. All three of these interests sought to maximize their respective control over the aboriginal populations. Outright enslavement of the Indians was the method preferred by the colonists. But neither the Crown nor the Church could permit this to happen without surrendering their own vested and potential interests in the greatest resource of the New World — its manpower.

Why then did they permit and even encourage the enslavement of Africans? In this matter, all three power groups stood to gain. Africans who remained in Africa were of no use to anybody, since effective military and political domination of that continent by Europeans was not achieved until the middle of the nineteenth century. To make use of African manpower, the Africans had to be removed from their homelands. The only way to accomplish this was to buy them as slaves from dealers on the coast. For both the Crown and the Church, it was better to have Africans under the control of the New World colonists than to have Africans under the control of nobody but Africans. This was especially true since the Negro slaves were destined primarily for the use of lowland planters. The importation of slaves from Africa would therefore not interfere with the *modus vivendi* worked out by Church, State and colonists in the highlands. On the contrary, the flow of Negro slaves to the lowlands helped to prevent competition between lowland planters and highland entrepreneurs for control over highland labor.

The success of the clerics in the Court of Spain on behalf of the prohibition of Indian slavery is not to be attributed to their eloquence or to the passionate conviction which they conveyed to the Spanish monarchs. The laws of 1542 were passed because slavery of the highland Indians was a political and economic threat to the sovereignty of the Spanish Crown in the New World. There is no other way to explain the benevolent, pious concern exhibited on behalf of the Indians in contrast to the indifference displayed toward the Negroes.

The New Laws were thus essentially an attempt to prevent the formation of a feudal class in Spain's American territories. This threat had arisen out of the method employed by the Spanish Crown to reward the activities and exploits of its *conquistadores*. The astonishing, almost superhuman exploits of the Spanish invaders of the New World were motivated by the promise of extraordinary privileges with respect to the lands and peoples whom they were able to conquer. Although the privilege of taking slaves was of considerable importance in the system of rewards in the lowland regions, outright slavery was a relatively minor aspect of the rewards system in the highlands. In the highlands a much more effective system was employed as the dominant form of labor appropriation. This system was known as the *encomienda*. Its salient feature was that a man who had performed service on behalf of the Crown in the conquest of the new territories was rewarded with the privilege of collecting tribute and drafting labor among a stated group of Indians inhabiting a particular set of villages. Cortes, for example, received an *encomienda* consisting of twenty-two townships, inhabited by possibly as many as 115,000 people.[14] The Crown was aware of the fact that such grants of privileges amounted to the establishment of a feudal noble class in the New World and hence it sought to diminish the resemblance between the *encomienda* and feudalism by hedging the grant with various restrictions. For example, theoretically the right of administering justice was to be reserved to Crown officials and to be removed from the sphere of the *encomendero*'s authority. It was intended, in other words, that the Indians should remain subjects of the Crown, not of the *encomendero*. The *encomendero* was merely to have the privilege of assigning work duties to the Indians in his *encomienda* or of collecting tribute from them.

Despite these provisions, however, the great *encomenderos*, such as Cortes in Mexico and Pizarro in Peru, quickly acquired the *de facto* status of full feudal lords, exercising almost unrestricted, despotic control over the populations within their *encomiendas*. In practice it was impossible for the Crown and its representatives in the New World to enforce the safeguards of the *encomienda* system. Hence, the New Laws constituted a package of proposals designed to pry loose the *encomienda* and slave Indians from the tenacious grasp of the *encomenderos* and slaveholders. The laws decreed that the Indians were to be regarded as free men and as vassals of the King of Spain. They sought to prevent the inheritance of existing *encomiendas* and to reduce those of excessive dimensions. Mistreatment of the Indians, their enslavement or excessive brutality toward them were to be punished very severely. When the Crown attempted to enforce these laws in Peru and Panama, it provoked outright rebellions. As is frequently the case in colonial situations, the power of the metropolitan forces was unequal to the power, ingenuity and perseverance of the colonizers who were in direct contact with the native peoples.

Although it is true that the Spanish Crown was largely successful in eliminating Indian slavery, it must be understood that such a statement depends on a highly technical definition of slavery. The *encomienda* and the other systems of compulsory labor which followed it during the colonial and republican periods were certainly markedly different from the arrangement worked out for labor on the lowland tropical plantations. I shall try to describe these differences in a moment, but one must never lose sight of the fact that all through the colonial, republican and modern periods in the history of highland Latin America, the Indian population has been subjected to one form or another of compulsory labor.

As the Crown promulgated and attempted to enforce the laws against the *encomienda* system, it introduced a new method of labor use. This system, known as *mit'a* in Peru, *minga* in Ecuador, *catequil* or *repartimiento* in Mexico, and *mandamiento* in Guatemala, was introduced about the middle of the sixteenth century. By 1600, it had become the dominant form of labor recruitment in highland Latin America.[15] The *repartimiento* substituted Crown officials for the *encomendero* as the principal agent for labor recruitment purposes. These Crown officials were alone empowered to draw upon the labor resources of the Indian villages. Theoretically, even the owners of *encomiendas* now had to consult the royal administrators and judges with respect to the allocation of laborers on their own *encomiendas*. Although the officials in charge of labor recruitment were instructed to take precautions designed to protect the health and well-being of the Indians under their jurisdiction, there were naturally frequent abuses and disregard of the letter of the law. Private entrepreneurs undoubtedly approached the officials and curried their favor with bribes and gifts in order to avail themselves of the Indian labor under the officials' control. The result was that the *repartimiento* reform did not result in any substantial improvement from the point of view of the Indian laborers. Their situation, in effect, remained unchanged. Indeed, their plight continued to resemble pre-contact times when the rulers of the native states had carried out periodic drafts of Indian labor through the system of the aboriginal *mit'a*. Instead of a native nobility, there were now the representatives of the Spanish Crown and the private entrepreneurs who exercised the right to draw on the manpower of the Indian villages.

The *repartimiento* was probably the cheapest form of labor that has ever been invented. To begin with, and unlike slavery, the system required no initial investment of capital. True, the Crown insisted that the labor drafts be paid wages, but these wages, when they were not withheld through fraud and chicanery, were a caricature of a genuine wage system. In many instances, their only function was to permit the Indian to pay taxes to the Crown. Unlike the wages extended to even the most defenseless urban proletariat, their level was set below what was necessary to maintain the life of the workers. Indeed, this was the great advantage of the *repartimiento*. Like the modern systems of migratory labor which still exist in Mozambique and Angola, the *repartimiento* exempted the employer from any concern with the subsistence requirements of his employees.[16] This effect was achieved by permitting or compelling the work force to labor in its own *milpas* (farms) for most of the year, from whence came the food by which it subsisted and reproduced itself. In this context, the endlessly repeated refrain, common to both Africa and the New World, that the natives are lazy and do not voluntarily work for wages, acquires a peculiarly poisonous sting. In general, the highland Indian simply could not convert to full-time wage labor and eat at the same time. As J. Phelan has said, "The stereotype that the white man found he could not bribe the Indian to work for a wage and so resorted to one form or another of compulsion is false. With alacrity, the Indians took to earning a living in European fashion when they were adequately compensated."[17]

Throughout the colonial period, there were institutions at work which directly and indirectly pressured the Indians both to increase their involvement in this bastard form of wage labor and to convert part of their own agricultural product into money. The greater the involvement of the Indians in a cash economy, the more opportunities there were for other sectors of the colonial population, especially the Church and the mestizo trading class, to share the benefits enjoyed by the agricultural and industrial entrepreneurs who depended on native labor. It was to the economic advantage of everybody except the Indians, in other words, that the Indians enter the market economy to the maximum extent compatible with their primary assignment as subsistence farmers. The famous highland "fiesta complex," to be discussed in the next chapter, was one of the central devices by which this involvement was heightened. The more general ingredient in this peculiar labor syndrome was the system which permitted employers to compel Indians to discharge debts through labor services. This device was introduced at least as early as the *repartimiento*. But it was destined to acquire supreme importance during the nineteenth century in the form of debt peonage. Why this came about, we shall see in a moment.

As part of its plan to retain direct control over the Indian population, the Spanish Crown, throughout the colonial period, systematically gathered the Indians into nucleated villages called *reducciones* or *congregaciones*. Such nucleation was potentially of advantage to all three elements — Church, colonists and Crown — concerned with making profitable use of the aborigines. But the Crown did not stop at merely establishing villages. It insisted that not only ought the Indians to be gathered together, but that land be given to villages under communal tenure. Worse, from the viewpoint of the colonists, these lands were declared inviolable. They could neither be sold nor pawned. As a result of this aspect of Crown policy — one of the most fascinating counterpoints in the long colonial fugue — many fertile and well-watered lands remained in native hands until the nineteenth century. Needless to say, these lands were coveted by the *hacendados*.

In a remarkably parallel fashion, all through the highland area, one of the first actions of the nineteenth-century republican governments, after independence had been achieved from Spain, was the destruction of the safeguards preventing direct access to Indian land and labor. In the name of liberal ideologies, elevating the principle of private property and individual rights to supreme consideration, the governments of the newly established highland republics one after the other decreed the end of the communal land system. All communal properties (including those of the Church) had to be converted into private holdings. Since this conversion required legal expertise, the *hacendados* experienced no great difficulty in gaining title to the Indian properties. What the lawyers could not grab for them, they took by force. The result was that by the end of the nineteenth century practically every acre of high-quality land in Mexico, Guatemala, Ecuador, Peru and Bolivia was part of a white man's or mestizo's *hacienda*.

What happened to the Indians who had lived in these areas? For the most part, they remained in place, since the *hacendados* as usual wanted both the land *and* the labor. Having possession of one, it was easy to obtain the other. The landless Indian now had no choice. He could only gain his subsistence by working for some *hacendado*. This much was guaranteed, but which *hacendado* was it to be? The *haciendas* (which, incidentally, now that the Crown was out of the picture, had begun to attract foreign capital) could ill afford to permit the development of a mobile, free-floating agricultural proletariat. The laborers had to be fixed in one place if maximum use was to be made of them. The device needed to accomplish this was already present.

22

Food and clothing were advanced to the Indians, and wages were set at a point low enough to insure that the debts could never be discharged. An Indian who had fallen into debt could not quit his job or leave the premises until the debt was liquidated. If a man died before his debt was paid, his children fell heir to the obligation. Thus it was that debt peonage replaced the *repartimiento* as the dominant mode of labor control.

This is not to say that other forms of forced labor more closely resembling the *repartimiento* entirely disappeared. On the contrary, numerous labor recruiting schemes based on arbitrary definitions of vagrancy, criminality and public welfare were prominent throughout the highlands, except for Mexico, well into the twentieth century. In Peru, Ecuador and Guatemala, they still enjoy a *de facto* if not legal existence. It is interesting to note that in Guatemala the influence of heavily capitalized coffee and banana plantations was sufficient to swing the pendulum almost all the way back to a system of the *repartimiento* variety. This happened when the center of agricultural production shifted to areas outside of the control of the nineteenth-century *haciendas*. In 1936, the dictator Ubico replaced debt slavery by a system based upon vagrancy, thereby prying loose the *peones* from the grasp of the older landed interests.[18]

Paradoxically, the removal of the Crown's protective shield from the corporate nucleated Indian villages did not result in the total destruction of the type. Throughout the highlands there survive to this day two distinct kinds of Indians. In the first instance there are Indians who are part of a permanent labor force residing on *haciendas*. In the second instance there are Indians who live in "free" villages. The latter are usually located in the commercially worthless lands adjacent to *haciendas*, on hillsides, or in other areas which were of little use to the *hacendados* during their nineteenth-century rampage.

As Eric Wolf has suggested, the perpetuation of these free Indian communities was to a large extent a pattern thoroughly consistent with the needs of the *hacienda* system,[19] especially in its more heavily capitalized phases in the late nineteenth and present centuries. Since the amount of land permitted the free Indian villages was strictly limited and of inferior quality, the inhabitants remained responsive to labor requests from the *hacendados*. These free villagers were also made debtors to the *hacendados* but by more subtle and intermittent methods. They thus constituted a reserve labor pool which could be drawn upon for intensive harvesting operations and for the construction of roads, canals and other public works.[20]

What Wolf fails to make sufficiently clear is that no genuine equivalents of these highland Indian villages are to be found in any of the New World's lowland plantation areas. In lowland Latin America, the same array of powers — Crown, Church and colonists — had also been struggling for the control of cheap labor. In the lowlands, however, the balance struck was earlier and more heavily in favor of the colonists. The virtual extinction of the Indians, and the importation of Africans as slaves, meant the triumph of the colonists over Church and State. Each plantation was a political microcosm in which the slaves were ruled by an absolute despot, their owner. In this context, the development of a corporate village organization similar to that of the highland communities was clearly out of the question. The plantation was the typical lowland form of community. Out from the plantation, with its heavy capital investment, its concentration on single commercial crops, and its sensitivity to world market prices, there flowed a fundamentally different kind of peasant culture and racial prospectus. This contrast between lowland and highland community types is fundamental for an understanding of the contrast between highland and lowland race relations. It will be appropriate, therefore,, to take a closer look at the cultural and social heritage of the two labor systems as they are embodied in community life.

3 / The Highland Heritage

The distinctive highland Indian villages to which I have been referring have been classified by Eric Wolf as examples of the closed-corporate-peasant community. According to Wolf, the distinctive feature of these communities is that there is communal control of landholdings either through common ownership or by community-imposed sanctions against sale to outsiders. The interest in protecting the community land leads to a life which is saturated by participation in communal political and religious affairs. Other related diagnostics listed by Wolf include a tendency for an intimate interplay to take place between political and religious activities; an emphasis on prestige derived from community display; culturally recognized standards of consumption which consciously exclude cultural alternatives; defensive ignorance; a pattern of rejection of novelty; a cult of poverty; and a system of institutionalized envy leading to the restriction of consumption standards and the leveling of intra-communal economic differences.[1]

In the highland Indian closed-corporate-peasant communities from Mexico to Bolivia, the distinctive features of the type are best illustrated through the complex of institutions known as the fiesta system. All Indian men are expected to take part in this system. In their youth they are obliged to assume certain menial offices or *cargos*, that is, "burdens," such as carrying messages for the councilmen, serving on the night watch, or cleaning the church. Eventually, each man is obliged to "volunteer" for a major *cargo*.

This involves organizing and carrying out the fiesta of one of the saints who is traditionally regarded as especially significant in the life of the village. As a man moves up through this hierarchy of religious obligations, he is rewarded with increasing amounts of prestige. In addition, everywhere among the corporate Indian villages, satisfaction of religious burdens leads to or is accompanied by parallel progress up a ladder of political offices such as sheriff, councilman, mayor, etc. Thus, the *principales,* or top-ranking Indian personalities, are always individuals who have had a distinguished record as fiesta-givers and civil office holders.

The burdensome aspect of the *cargos* and political offices is that they involve considerable expenditure of time and money. Fiestas are costly affairs since large quantities of food and drink (especially drink) must be dispensed. In addition, the cost of special church services, candles, costumes for dancers and players, musicians, fireworks, bulls and bullfighters, and many other festive items must also be met. In the classic stereotype, it is alleged that the *carguero,* or burden-bearer, frequently cannot meet these expenses out of his normal income and must borrow from friends and relatives, sell or pawn land, or otherwise place himself in debt for a considerable period. "Generally, the higher offices in the hierarchy are the most costly, and economic ruin, at least temporarily, accompanies the acquired social prestige."[2] In order to meet his burden an Indian will ". . . spend all he has, go into debt, and sell his labor for trifling wages even though he ends in virtual slavery."[3]

Many anthropologists view the fiesta complex of the corporate villages as essentially a survival of allegedly aboriginal non-Western notions of economic utility and self-interest. The Indians entertain themselves, gain prestige and venerate the saints by giving the fiestas, and this is to them a more "rational" use of money than investing it in land, livestock, machinery or education. After all, what is so strange about squandering one's money on a good time? Only people suffering from a "Protestant ethic" find this a problem worth bothering about. On the other hand, there are many anthropologists who feel that the fiesta system *is* a bit "odd" and that it *does* demand a serious explanation. There are several reasons why the "burdens" simply cannot be dismissed as an example of the whimsical and quixotic (to us) things which men will do in order to achieve prestige.

First of all, recent studies have confirmed what had long been suspected about the origin of the fiesta system's ritual content, namely that it is almost wholly sixteenth-century Spanish-Catholic. Therefore, to talk about aboriginal survivals in this context is clearly out of the question.[4] Secondly, and more important, the irrational, uneconomic aspects of fiesta behavior stand in marked contrast to the economic individualism, constant penny-pinching and obsessive involvement with price which is one of the most pronounced features of highland Indian life. So conspicuous is the highland Indian's dedication to the principles of thrift, investment and *caveat emptor* that Sol Tax was moved to call the Indians of Panajachel, Guatemala, "penny capitalists."[5] In the Zapotec town in Mexico, Elsie Clews Parsons was overwhelmed by the same pattern: "Mitla is a business town. Trade permeates its whole life; price is of supreme interest to young and old, women and men, the poor and well to do."[6] Once, when Parsons had finished telling a group of Indians how one of her relatives had died in a motorcycle accident, the first question which the Indians put to her was: "How much does a motorcycle cost?" In Yalalag, another Zapotecan village, Julio de la Fuente also gives a picture of total involvement in petty commercial activities. Here the penny-pinching is so obsessive that "brothers cheat each other,"[7] families break up over debts,[8] and "to ask for loans among relatives is frowned upon because they suspect that you are not going to repay them."[9]

The attempt to explain the fiesta complex has recently focused on the needs of the corporate Indian community to level internal wealth differences as a protective device. Wolf, for example, implies that the political-religious-prestige interplay is an aspect of the community's attempt to increase its internal solidarity in defense of the land.[10] In a somewhat similar vein, but without bothering with a material base, C. Leslie has suggested that Mitla's fiesta system is a check upon the destructive individualistic tendencies of the Mitleños. The townspeople complain about the burdens of the fiesta system, but according to Leslie, the vision that there could conceivably be "no law other than their desires, no limit other than that which they think advisable" inhibits would-be critics of saint's festivals and causes them to go unheeded in the community at large. "Thus families with the values of the market place, and priding themselves as experts in following its competitive ways, Mitleños nonetheless subordinated themselves ... to ideals of proper conduct which disabused all but the most obdurate individuals of the notion that they might live wholeheartedly in pursuit of their own self-interest."[11]

The difficulty with viewing the fiesta complex as an egalitarian device of the corporate peasant community is twofold: First of all, although the fiesta system does tend to place an upper limit upon the amount of capital which an individual Indian can accumulate, it has never prevented the formation of rather sharp socio-economic differences within the Indian communities. There is very little evidence to support the stereotyped version of the *cargo* which causes "economic ruin." In Charles Wagley's Santiago Chimaltenango and Ruth Bunzel's Chichicastenango it was specifically established that most of the people are too poor to be able to afford the major *cargos*.[12] According to La Farge, the civil-religious leaders are "in almost every village ... extremely prosperous."[13] Marked differences in wealth among Indians is also characteristic of Tepotzlan (especially before the revolution), Mitla and Yalalag, and many other, if not all highland Indian communities which have been studied by anthropologists.[14]

I do not mean to say that the fiesta system never forces any Indians into debt. The tendency of this form of conspicuous consumption to induce many Indians to spend more than their resources allow is, as we shall see, a very important function of the system in relationship to peonage and migratory labor. The point is that the *cargos* do not bring economic ruin to everyone. Many of the most burdensome fiestas are underwritten precisely by those people who are best able to afford them. To a *principal* or *cacique*, the *cargos* were not economically fatal. Indeed they were *principales* and *caciques* — "big shots" — precisely because, unlike lesser mortals, they were able to buy enough *aguardiente* for the whole village to get drunk, without having to sell their lands and animals, and without having to work on a "foreigner's" *hacienda*.

Not only has the fiesta system failed to level the Indians into a homogeneous solidary group, but a more inefficient defense against outsiders could scarcely be imagined. It might be argued that the fiesta system has helped to maintain the separate identity of the highland communities, but this is scarcely a result which possesses any clear adaptive advantages for the members of such communities. On the contrary, these communities themselves are the product of a colonial policy whose net result in the long run was the maintenance of the Indians in an "exploited and degraded condition." Far from protecting the Indian communities against *encomienda, repartimiento,* debt peonage, excessive taxation and tribute, the fiesta system was an integral and enduring part of the mechanisms by which these noxious influences gained access to the very heart of the village.

It seems all too often to be forgotten that the closed corporate villages fulfilled certain vital functions with respect to the larger system in which Indian life was embedded. From the point of view of this larger system the proliferation of ceremonies, the burdens of the *cargueros,* and the whole civil-religious hierarchy are nothing but direct or indirect expressions of the economic and political vassalage into which the Indians have fallen. Consider, for example, the way in which one village is closed off from other villages. All observers of highland Indian life agree that an extraordinary degree of local ethnocentrism characterizes these communities. This quaint, introverted focus, expressed in endogamy, distinctive patterns of dress, speech and other customs so dear to the hearts of certain anthropologists, has another side to it. Was this not exactly what was needed in order to stave off for the longest possible time the ultimate hour of reckoning that comes to every political system which mercilessly degrades and exploits its human resources?[15] Again, it is no accident that the Indian leader who emerges from the fiesta system is typically one who has no authority beyond his own locality. The highlands had passed beyond the village level of socio-cultural organization at least a thousand years before the Europeans arrived. What else then is the closed-corporate-peasant community, if not an artifact created by the invaders to make certain that the state level of organization would never again fall under Indian control?

Also, it is all too frequently forgotten that in terms of the colonial system, the fiesta complex was a direct expression of the attempt by the Church to maintain control over the highland Indian populations and to derive wealth from them. Although this situation has been drastically modified in many highland countries today, it was clearly a dominant factor in the fiesta complex at least as far back as the eighteenth century. The famous report of Antonio de Ulloa, who was sent out by the Spanish Crown to investigate conditions in eighteenth-century Peru, contains a clear statement of the functions which the fiesta system played in relationship to the maintenance of Church income. Ulloa was astonished by the number of saint's days which were celebrated in the highland Indian villages. He noted that one of the first tasks which a newly appointed priest undertook was to create additional fiestas, requiring additional outlays for various services rendered by the Church and its representatives. Speaking of the *mayordomos* upon whom the burden of the fiesta rested, Ulloa noted that by the Indian's participation in the celebration of the saint's day, he was relieved "of all the money which he had been able to collect during the whole year and also all the fowls and animals which his wife and children have reared in their huts, so that his family is left destitute of food and reduced to wild herbs and to the grains which they cultivate in their small gardens."[16]

To become a *carguero* was far from being a spontaneous undertaking stimulated by deep religious feeling and a sense of obligation. Ulloa observed that many of the *cargueros* were simply forced into the position of underwriting the fiesta by command from the priest. "As soon as the sermon of the day is concluded, the curate reads a paper on which he has inscribed names of those who are to be masters of ceremonies for the festivals of the following year, and if anyone does not accept it of his free will, he is forced to give his consent by dint of blows. And when his day comes there is no apology that can exonerate him from having the money ready."[17]

The intimate relationship between the local priest, the village Indian hierarchy, the fiesta system, Church finance and politico-economic control is still clearly visible. In 1960, I had the opportunity to live in an Indian village in Chimborazo Province, Ecuador, and to observe aspects of the modern fiesta system for three months. In Ecuadorian Indian villages, nominations for the fiesta leader are submitted to the parish priest by Indian officials residing within the village. These officials are instructed by the priest, as well as by the local representative of the state, the *teniente político,* to identify Indians in their village who have given evidence during the past year of being able to support the financial burden of the fiesta. Acting on this information, the priest, backed up by the *teniente político,* appoints the new *cargueros* at the mass on the fiesta of the saint's day.[18]

True enough, direct physical coercion is not used as it was when Ulloa observed the system. Nonetheless, the threat of material sanctions does not lie far behind the façade of persuasion and voluntary accommodation. The *teniente político* exercises great discretionary powers in relation to the adjudication of land claims, as well as in all processes of a legal nature requiring paperwork and reference to higher authority. Indians who are uncooperative with respect to the fiesta system earn a bad reputation among the authorities external to the village and they are subject to harassment in the form of excessive obligations placed on them for community labor and to unfair treatment in litigation.

According to Núñez del Prado, today in the Andes, "It should be noted that men very rarely volunteer for a *cargo.* In most cases a man is chosen against his will and persuaded to accept it when he is drunk."[19] A poignant description of what appears to be a similar situation is provided by Ruth Bunzel for Guatemala:

The conventional behavior for candidates for all offices is to refuse to serve, and to have the office thrust on them. Sometimes physical force is used in forcing the insignia of office upon unwilling candidates. At the feast of Santo Tomas I saw the candidates for office for the coming year being dragged forcibly through the streets, kicking and struggling. I saw one of the newly chosen *regidores* (councilmen) bolt for the door, after he had been brought in, like a prisoner, for the notification. All the *regidores* and *mayores* were on hand, armed with sticks to prevent the escape of the candidates. It took over an hour to persuade the candidate for First Alcade [mayor] to accept the nomination.[20]

It should also be noted that the contemporary system depends to a great extent upon the consensus among the members of the Indian village that those who shirk their burdens as *cargueros* ought not to receive the respect to which those who have accepted the burden are entitled. If one has given a fiesta and suffered the economic consequences, he does not view with equanimity the prospect of others in the village failing to assume their proper share of the burden. Thus, a good deal of the pressure for the maintenance of the system apparently arises spontaneously from within the Indian village itself. However, this is a superficial interpretation of the forces which are at work. At the outset, to follow Antonio de Ulloa's lead, the fiestas functioned primarily to drain off a portion of the community's wealth in support of the Church bureaucracy. At the same time, the associated civil-religious hierarchy was a tool of the colonial government. The *caciques* and *principales* were puppet leaders who in return for collaboration in the work of recruiting for *mit'a* and *catequil* were vested with some semblance of local authority and power. In this context, it should be mentioned that one of the major rewards of officeholding has always been exemption from forced labor.

In modern times the draining of community wealth through the mechanism of the fiesta system is no longer primarily destined to benefit the Church. In the nineteenth century, during the course of the establishment of the liberal republican regimes, the Church suffered serious setbacks and was reduced to a position of secondary importance in the control of Indian communities. After the passing of restrictive legislation and the expropriation of Church lands, the Church ceased to be the primary direct economic beneficiary of the fiesta system. This position was now taken over by the *haciendas* and the *hacendado* class and the fiesta system became an integral part of the mechanisms by which Indians, during the nineteenth and twentieth centuries, were enticed into debt on behalf of the system of debt peonage.

Left to their own devices, the Indians were perfectly capable of maintaining a level of consumption realistically adjusted to the marginal wages which their labor commanded. The fiesta system, however, compelled them periodically to acquire goods on a scale which was far above their normal needs. In Guatemala, as recently as the 1930's, the fiesta system was deliberately used by the *haciendas* to recruit Indian labor. *Hacienda* agents were sent out to scour the countryside for prospective workers for the plantations. These labor recruiters sought out the holders of *cargos* and offered loans on deceptively friendly terms.[21] In addition, it is clear from numerous community studies carried out in the highland region that the non-Indian sectors of the population, in general, stand to gain from a continuation of the fiesta system, since the celebration of fiestas provides the principal occasion for the purchase of non-subsistence goods. Wagley's comment, "These days are very lucrative for the Ladinos of Chimaltenango," is applicable to most highland fiestas.[22] Generally speaking, throughout the highland region, fiesta buying involves the Indians in transactions with non-Indians who control the commercial sources of non-subsistence commodities. The entire non-Indian sector of the highland countries, therefore, maintains a powerful vested interest in the preservation of the fiesta system. The system prevents the rise of genuine native leaders, because it drains off the excess wealth of Indians, cutting short the prospects for the accumulation of capital resources among the Indians in the village. The wealth that is drained off is used to support the Church hierarchy and to stimulate the entrance of the Indian into the extra-village labor market. It is also used as a stimulant to raise the consumption standards among the Indians and hence to increase the rate of commercial transactions between non-Indians and Indians.

Those who doubt the fundamentally repressive and abusive character of the classic fiesta complex should compare the celebration of fiestas in Indian communities with the manner in which devotion to saints is practiced in non-Indian villages. Moche, a mestizo community in Peru, also has many saint's days. The people of Moche become *cargueros*, and they give relatively expensive fiestas. However, the *carguero* in the non-Indian community is not at all subject to the financial burdens which must be shouldered by the Indian *carguero*. On the contrary, the fiesta is viewed in Moche as a means by which the saints may be venerated and the pocket of the *carguero* swelled. Far from incurring crushing financial losses, the Moche *cargueros* emerge from the fiesta with a handsome profit. This profit is gained by soliciting financial contributions from all of the townspeople as well as from people living in the surrounding area, and by carefully gearing expenses to income.[23] Thus, although the non-Indian fiestas are phrased in a fashion quite similar to that characteristic of the Indian fiestas, the primary functional significance is drastically different. No Moche *carguero* ever needs to be dragged screaming through the streets to the ceremony of his installation.

I have, perhaps, failed to make adequately clear that the Indian's burden in the fiesta system is not restricted merely to the expenses which must be met in the course of carrying out the celebration of the saint's day; the really critical involvement may in certain cases be the necessity of devoting most of the year to the performance of the secular duties which the *carguero* is also expected to assume. In the classic form of the Indian fiesta system, appointees to *cargos* are automatically expected to serve in the village council. This requires their presence in the village away from their farms for a good portion of the year, and in many cases represents a greater sacrifice than the actual expenses of the fiesta. This aspect of the fiesta system also tends to be absent among the non-Indian communities.

It should be mentioned that many non-Indian fiesta complexes in Latin America do not derive their principal impetus from the entrepreneurial advantages accruing to the specific individuals who undertake the fiesta. There is also a very widespread pattern in which the fiesta is essentially geared to the marketing and commercial requirements of the mestizo or *ladino* community as a whole. Under such circumstances, the fiesta is advertised by the *ladino* town council in neighboring communities, and the spectacular nature of the proposed entertainments and festivities is offered as an attraction for the largest possible number of visitors to the community on the saint's day. These fiestas are really fairs, designed to stimulate the commercial life of the town, or to make the town conspicuous in the hope that its products will achieve widespread popularity. Under such circumstances, the fiesta is merely an adjunct of the market. For example, in the community of Tzintzuntzan, located in highland Mexico, the day of the town's most important fiesta is likewise the day on which the greatest market is held; since the people of Tzintzuntzan specialize in making pottery, they are most eager to have the largest possible number of prospective buyers of their wares present at their fiestas. A considerable proportion of the town's annual ceramic output is sold to the 8,000 or so people who attend the great celebration of their town's patron saint.[24] One fact which has tended to obscure the functional analysis of the fiesta system in highland Latin America is that the pattern which I have been identifying especially with the mestizos or *ladinos* actually occurs among many Indian villages as well. This is particularly true of Mexico, where after the 1910-20 Revolution, political and religious reforms made it possible for the Indians more closely to approximate the position of the mestizos within the total national economy and polity.[25]

In addition to the fiesta complex, there are many other characteristics of the corporate villages which are part of the heritage of the colonial and republican systems for making use of the labor of the highland Indians. The Indians everywhere tend to occupy the more marginal lands; they tend to produce subsistence crops rather than commercial crops; they tend to have a higher rate of illiteracy; a higher rate of infant mortality; a shorter life expectancy; and a lower per capita income than the non-Indian populations of the countries they inhabit. Where Indians and *ladinos* or mestizos live in the same communities, the Indians tend to be politically subordinate, and they are subject in many instances to outright discrimination in terms of housing and social etiquette. For example, in highland Guatemalan communities, it is not unusual for Indians to be obliged to step off the street in order to make way for *ladinos*.[26] In rural highland Ecuador, it is expected that Indians will yield positions on public conveyances to *ladinos*,[27] and in Peru and Ecuador it is not rare for *hacendados*, in collaboration with the local police, to use brutal methods for the suppression of Indian "deviants." In Guatemala, there is segregation in housing, street corner gatherings, recreation and leisure, local and national fiestas, social visiting and friendship units, school functions, weddings, baptisms, wakes, funerals, eating and marriage.[28] Throughout the highland region, with the possible exception of certain social strata in Mexican urban centers, the *ladinos* or mestizos tend to regard the Indians as inferior creatures and harbor many derogatory stereotypes with respect to them. Speaking of Ecuador, Peru and Bolivia, Núñez del Prado notes that "in all three countries contempt for everything Indian is habitual. . . ."[29] In Guatemala the Indians are said to be "stupid," "without shame," "like children," "dishonest" and "not deserving of respect."[30] I believe it could easily be shown that all of these manifestations of prejudice and discrimination against Indians are consequences of the labor policies pursued since the conquest. Certainly, the central feature of this highland pattern of prejudice and discrimination is the application of harsh labor laws exclusively to Indians.

The pattern of prejudice and discrimination against the highland Indians bears certain resemblances to the system of race relations involving whites and Negroes in the United States. As in the United States, the population is sharply divided into two major groups, one of which is subject to flagrant mistreatment at the hands of the other. Furthermore, as is true of every society in which discrimination is practiced on a systematic and intensive scale, identity in the subordinate group(s) is firmly and unambiguously established in local daily life.[31] In the United States, one is either white or Negro, and in much of highland Latin America, one is either mestizo (*ladino, blanco,* according to the country) or Indian.[32]

The similarities between the two systems of race relations, however, do not extend much beyond this point. Several striking differences must be noted. In the first place, the two systems treat the half-castes or hybrids in diametrically opposed ways. In the United States, all persons with any demonstrable degree of Negro parentage, visible or not, fall into the subordinate caste, according to the principle which I have elsewhere labeled "hypo-descent."[33] This has meant that from a biological point of view, the whites in the United States have remained relatively "pure," while the Negroes have become genetically less and less like their African forebears. In the Latin American highlands, however, there has never been a time when the hybrid types were automatically lumped together with the Indian. True, there had been a time when the Crown was intent on clearly separating all three types, i.e., whites, mestizos and Indians, and on assigning special privileges and obligations to each. But this system was always more of a legal fiction than a social reality.[34] Ever since independence, the highland populations have consisted of two major groupings: Indians and non-Indians. (Negro slaves, in small numbers, would make a third group, the lowest caste of all.) The Indians were subject to the special legal disabilities relating to labor while the whites and mestizos enjoyed the benefits therefrom. The superordinate caste of non-Indians did not enjoy their superior status because they looked Caucasoid or could actually demonstrate only Caucasoid descent. On the contrary, many of those who escaped the worst features of the labor laws were genetically more Indian than the *principales* or *caciques* of the corporate villages. To be an Indian in the highlands, as we shall see in a moment, is to be someone who *lives* like an Indian.

Who then are the mestizos and *ladinos?* Mestizos and

ladinos are non-Indians. They are the lower, rural, peasant portion of the superordinate caste. But they are part of that caste, not outside of it. They are not to be thought of as structurally intermediate to the European group.[35] The labor laws did not apply in halfway measure to the mestizos;[36] nor did the mestizos live in communities which were halfway between Indian and European communities. Of course, marked difference in power and style of life prevailed among the various strata and rural and urban segments of the superordinate non-Indian caste. But as far as the dominant land and labor issues in the relationship between aboriginals and invaders were concerned, the lower segment — the mestizos — was structurally aligned with the higher segments: the European- and American-born Caucasoids. The only sense in which they were intermediate was in terms of color prejudice. Caucasoid physical features were generally preferred by all strata of the dominant caste; hence the more Indian-looking, the less desirable the mestizo type. This, however, did not prevent many non-Caucasoid individuals from rising high in the colonial and republican aristocracy, although the highest economic and political positions tended everywhere to be monopolized by persons who showed the least genetic debt to the Indians. Eventually, in Mexico, the upper and lower strata of the superordinate caste came into conflict and fought a class war in which the more Caucasoid elite was defeated. The result is that in modern Mexico many of the highest economic and political positions are now in the grasp of people who could pass for Indians, if there were any reason for them to do so.

Thus racial identity in the highlands is established on quite different premises from those in the United States. The highland Indians are not usually distinguishable from non-Indians simply on the basis of physical appearance. From a purely physical point of view, most of the highland Indians could easily be taken for *ladinos* or mestizos, since the latter possess a considerable amount of Indian genetic admixture, while equally substantial frequencies of Caucasoid genes are found among the "Indians." Instead of depending upon physical appearance, Indian racial identity flows from the fact that one lives in an Indian community, speaks an Indian language, speaks Spanish with an Indian accent, wears Indian-style clothing or participates in Indian-type fiestas. The status of being an Indian, in other words, is essentially a matter of behaving according to patterns which are locally recognized as being Indian specialties.

Another contrast is that it is possible to admit that one has an Indian ancestor and still regard oneself and be regarded by others as a non-Indian. (No one can admit Negro parentage in the United States without thereby affiliating himself with the Negro group.) Indeed, in upper-middle-class Mexico City, to have an Indian ancestor is a source of considerable pride. Elsewhere, however, it is a source of amusement, and mild depreciation. As Núñez del Prado suggests, "It is very nearly an insult to suggest to a mestizo that he has an Indian relative"; very nearly, but not quite.[37]

A corollary of this difference in the mode of establishing racial identity is that "passing" is based primarily upon exposure to similar cultural conditioning rather than upon intermarriage and genetic change. Theoretically, it should be easier to "pass" under these circumstances than when marked physical differences are backed up by a rigid descent rule. Such seems to have been the case for Mexico at least, where the percentage of Indians in the population has declined from almost 99 per cent in 1600 to less than 11.5 per cent in 1950. Since the total Mexican population has risen during the same period from about 2 million to over 30 million, without appreciable foreign immigration, it would seem likely that passing from Indian to mestizo status has been largely responsible for the failure of the Indian population to keep pace with the growth of the non-Indian sectors.[38] It is possible, however, that large-scale passing is a relatively recent phenomenon associated with the Mexican revolution and the destruction of the *hacendado* class. Elsewhere, the disparity between the enculturation experience of Indians and mestizos has led to a much slower change in the balance between the racial segments. Unfortunately this is one of the many aspects of Latin American race relations which have yet to be the object of systematic and quantitative research. Such research is needed before a clearer picture of the tendencies toward and the barriers against the assimilation of the highland Indian can be drawn. In some regions, as in central and northern Mexico, the assimilation of the Indian is proceeding at a very rapid rate, while in others, the corporate villages appear to be clinging to their Indian identity with great tenacity.

I would offer the hypothesis that these rates of assimilation reflect varying local disparities between lower-class mestizo and Indian standards of living. It must be remembered that all of highland Latin America is characterized by a rigid class structure among the mestizos themselves, in which the lower class leads a life no less degraded and precarious than that of the Indians. Although the highland Indians are surrounded by mestizo populations which in general tend to enjoy a superior standard of living, there are many specific local contexts in which the situation is reversed. In Mexico, for example, it has been estimated that at least 100,000 Indians live better than the bulk of the mestizos.[39] In Ecuador, the case of the Otavalo Indians is relevant; these people have become remarkably skilled in the manufacture and sale of woolen garments,[40] and their wares have acquired a national reputation. Indeed, Otavalo Indians have been seen selling their blankets as far away as Rio de Janeiro and Panama City. Under these circumstances it would seem highly unlikely that Indians would want to exchange their identity for that of mestizos. Among the Otavalos it is the other way around. Mestizo weavers have recently been trying to pass themselves off as Otavalo Indians. Apparently many Indians could, if they wished, abandon their native village, learn to speak Spanish, and dress in the costume of the mestizo and thereby pass into the mestizo or *ladino* group. But many prefer to remain Indians. Apparently the rate of passing is limited by the fact that in many instances there is very little improvement to be gained from such a transition.

Rather than compete with the mestizos for what must in any event be a very low rung on the ladder of the social hierarchy, many Indian communities seem to prefer instead to turn inward and to reduce social intercourse with people outside of their villages to the absolute minimum required by the fiesta system and by the apparatus of national government. It is in these intensely involuted highland Indian villages, withdrawn from effective participation in the life of the nation, that one finds the most drastic results of the 400 years of repressive systems to which the highland Indians have been subjected. Everybody who comes from outside the village, with the exception perhaps of the priest, is viewed as a potential threat to life and property. In the experience of these people everything that originates outside the village inevitably results in severe restriction of liberty and economic well-being. Many lay and professional observers forget that these fears are grounded in historical fact. It is not without historical justification that the Indians of highland Ecuador kill several census takers every time the national government attempts to count the villagers. The observer who is unfamiliar with the historical background of these villages is often perplexed by the reluctance of the Indians to accept medical and technical aid. But their caution is an adaptation that has resulted from 400 years of broken promises.

First came the *conquistadores* to liberate them from the oppressive rule of the native bureaucracy; the result was the *encomienda*. Then came the Crown, to liberate them from the oppression of the *encomienda;* the *repartimiento* followed. Then there followed the wars of independence and the promise of liberty; the result was the *hacienda* system and debt peonage. In modern times, with the abolition of formal debt peonage and the modification of the power of the *haciendas*, a considerable lapse in time must be expected before the Indians come to the point of fearlessly accepting the new offers of assistance which their national governments are now making.

Many persons in the employ of national and international development organizations are prone to regard the withdrawal of the Indians and their rejection of outside assistance as an indication of their infantilism or perversity. The friendly agronomist is rebuffed when he offers the Indians seedlings for reforestation. Why have the Indians driven him out of the village? Because they suspect, possibly with some substance in fact, that the ultimate results will be even worse than what they have now. After they have lavished care on the seedlings and after the trees have matured, how can they be sure that someone else will not come along and cut them down?

A case from highland Ecuador involving an offer of Merino sheep may perhaps illustrate this point. At first the Indians refused to listen to the advice of the foreign specialist who had been hired to improve the aboriginals' livestock. The native sheep were indeed scrawny, of little use for food, and producing only scanty amounts of wool. The specialist urged the Indians to interbreed their sheep with the sheep he would make available to them at no cost, and he promised that they would soon enjoy the benefits of animals at least twice as productive in terms of meat and wool. No one would take the offer. At last in one of the remoter villages a sole Indian who saw no danger in the situation yielded to the seductive proposition of the international expert and accepted several of the Merinos.

Returning to the village after a year had gone by, the expert was greeted by the usual shower of stones. At last, he managed to prevail upon the villagers to explain to him what had happened. It was as he had said; the sheep which had resulted from the cross with the Merino were twice as large and twice as woolly as the native flocks. They were in fact the finest sheep in the region. But this phenomenon had not gone unnoticed by the mestizos who lived in the valley below the community. They had driven up one night in a truck and had herded all of the poor fellow's sheep into it and driven off. The Indian who had departed from the ancestral patterns now found himself without any sheep at all.

Attempts to extend medical assistance to highland Indian villagers frequently result in similar disasters. With their long-established reluctance to enter into relationships with non-villagers, the Indians initially suspect the offers of medical assistance and refuse to reveal who is sick. In desperation, however, when the patient is near the point of death, the villagers will avail themselves of the offer of medical help. The doctor is then presented with a case in advanced stages of deterioration and he urges the immediate removal of the

Indian to a hospital. In a high proportion of the cases such treatment is followed by the death of the patient and the spread of the myth that the hospital is a place to which the whites take Indians to die. Even when the doctor finally manages to gain the confidence of the village and is permitted to see patients whose disease is not in a terminal phase, the results are frequently unenviable. The doctor prescribes a remedy which can be purchased only at the drugstore. The drugstore, however, may be anywhere from 10 to 20 miles distant from the village. The drugs are expensive. The trip is costly in time lost from the work of the fields. But the hope of relieving the suffering of his loved one persuades the Indian to depart from his better judgment. He trudges off to town, buys the medicine and returns. He administers the medicine according to directions. When the bottle is empty he stops. The patient grows worse and dies. The next time the doctor appears, which may be anywhere from a month to half a year later, his inquiry about the welfare of the villagers is greeted by silence or else by fervent assurances that no one in the village is sick.

During 1960 a campaign was mounted in Chimborazo Province, Ecuador, to inoculate 80 per cent of the Indian villagers in the hope of eradicating smallpox. The vaccination teams were greeted in some of the villages with stones; in others they entered unmolested, only to find the houses abandoned and the Indians fled to the hills. In some villages, success was achieved only by prevailing upon the parish priest to invite the unsuspecting Indians to attend a special Mass. When everyone had entered the church, the doors were locked and the inoculations were started. Still unable to obtain the 80 per cent necessary for eliminating the disease as an endemic feature of the area, teams of vaccinators, sometimes disguised as Indians, took up stations in the various markets of the region. When an Indian passed whom they suspected of not having been treated, they seized him, and by force, if necessary, proceeded with the inoculation. This produced the counter-intelligence among the Indians who had yet to be inoculated that the whites, no longer satisfied with the theft of Indian lands and Indian waters, were now attempting to steal their blood.

4 / Plantation Heritage

The fundamental difference between the lowland and highland labor systems was the respective amount of capital invested in profit-making enterprises. The lowland labor force, for reasons previously elaborated, consisted of slaves whose purchase price had to include the costs of African wars and of ocean transport. Each plantation worker therefore represented a capital outlay not inferior to that invested in a fairly expensive piece of machinery. In addition, especially on the sugar plantations, a considerable investment in oxen, horses, carts, plows, machetes, milling machines, furnaces, cauldrons and other refinery equipment was also required. Then there were the "big house," the slave quarters, the artisan sheds, the large kitchens, the roads and wharfs. All of this, plus the land and the cane that grew on it, was the property of the plantation master. No priests or *corregidores* had a right to tell him what to do with any part of it. Even more than the early *encomiendas*, the plantation was an empire in miniature. "The mill-owner was well named the *señor de ingenio* or 'lord of the plantation' for he was in fact nearly absolute master in his own land."[1]

It was the amount of capital invested in the plantation which set it off from the classic version of the highland *hacienda*. The latter as defined by Wolf and Mintz is an

> ... agricultural estate operated by a dominant land owner and a dependent labor force organized to supply a small-scale market by means of scarce capital, in which the factors of production are employed not only for capital accumulation but also to support the status aspirations of the owner.

44

Plantations on the other hand

> ... are agricultural estates operated by dominant owner(s) (usually a corporation) and a dependent labor force, organized to supply a large-scale market by means of abundant capital, in which the factors of production are employed primarily to further capital accumulation without reference to status needs of the owners.[2]

Actually, plantations and *haciendas* should probably be thought of as the polar extremes of a taxonomic continuum. The more heavily capitalized the agricultural estate, the larger the market for its product, and the more intensively it applies men, machinery and land to the production of a single crop, the closer it will be to Wolf and Mintz's model. It is clear that the colonial sugar plantations were only midway along this continuum since they were not at the outset anonymous corporations: master-slave relations were heavily personalized and status aspirations were certainly an important component in the owner's decision-making processes. Charles Wagley and I have called this early version of the plantation the *engenho* plantation, and distinguish it from the *usina* plantation, or "factory in the field" polar extreme:

> The center of the [*engenho*] plantation, and of the community or neighborhood which it formed, was the mansion in which the owner, his large family, and the many domestic servants lived. A chapel, which was either attached to the mansion or situated near it, served as the church for the owners and for the slave workers. ... Characteristically, the plantation settlement pattern was a concentrated one resembling that of a small village. ... On the average, no more than 200 to 300 people lived on a relatively large [*engenho*] sugar plantation, and within this small village-like society social relations tended to be intimate and highly personal.[3]

The heavier capital investment of the *engenho* as compared with that of the highland *hacienda* meant that the productive processes had to be much more systematized, with work allocation following rationally planned and closely inspected routines. The colonial highland *haciendas,* on the other hand, rarely concentrated on the production of a single commercial crop. Instead, probably the bulk of the labor effort was invested in a variety of food crops with which the resident labor force attempted to feed itself. Indeed, work specifically for the owner was sometimes restricted to only two or three days a week and to periodic calls for tours of house-service. In contrast, so valuable was the labor of the slave in relationship to the owner's investment in land and machinery that he frequently could not be spared for subsistence food production. In *The Masters and the Slaves,* Gilberto Freyre has given us a vivid account of the Brazilian sugar coast's food problems:

> Neither beef nor mutton nor even chicken was to be had. Neither fruits nor vegetables.... Such beef as was to be found was lean, the cattle coming from far away in the backlands with no pasturage to refresh them after their long journey.... Those oxen and cows that were not employed in agricultural service were looked upon as damned by the owners of the big estates.[4]

The business of the sugar plantations was to grow and refine sugar; that of the *haciendas* was to grow enough food to feed the *peones* and the *hacendado's* family. The relatively small surplus then went for the purchase of consumer luxuries. In many instances, the *haciendas* were simply village communities which had been captured and preserved by the *hacendado.* The slave plantation, however, was a radical ecological innovation. Far from incorporating or preserving native communities within its borders or adjacent to its margins, the plantation obliterated every vestige of aboriginal village life not only in its immediate vicinity but for hundreds of miles into the interior. Moreover, although it replaced the native Indian population several times over with imported Negroes, its *raison d'être* was absolutely contrary to transplanting African forms of community organization. Thus, the plantation had no use for, and indeed was inimical to, the existence of the highland types of closed corporate villages. Wagley has recently summed up this situation as follows:

The lack of a strong and well-defined local community in the Caribbean region is the result of slavery and a plantation economy. The decimation of the Indians in the region precluded any possible aboriginal basis for local community life. . . . Under Caribbean conditions, the Spanish, English, Dutch and French all proved unable to install successfully communities patterned on those of the mother country, as was done in parts of Mexico and Guatemala. The plantation headquarters overshadowed the towns which served as administrative and political centers. . . .While paternalism and common residence often united the slaves of a particular plantation into a neighborhood, they were unable to develop a full community life. Even after abolition the plantation system continued to exert an influence unfavorable to the development of a strong and cohesive local community. As T. Lynn Smith has pointed out, Brazil, and to a certain extent, the southern United States, share this historical heritage of the plantation and slavery and the resulting weak, divided and amorphous community. One is tempted to generalize that wherever the plantation and slave system were present, the rural community could not become an efficient and cohesive social unit.[5]

The plantation system and the absence of the corporate peasant village are in turn correlated with a large number of additional divergent cultural developments in the two regions. In both the highlands and the lowlands, the labor systems acted as filters through which only certain of the aboriginal cultural patterns were permitted to pass. Consider for example the vitality exhibited by the highland American Indian languages. In Peru, Bolivia and Ecuador as many people speak Indian languages as speak Spanish. In marked contrast, nowhere in the lowland regions has an African language survived intact. This is not to say that African speech patterns did not have an effect upon the language spoken by the conquerors. Brazilian Portuguese and lowland Spanish are markedly different from the languages of the mother countries and undoubtedly it was the influence of African phonetic patterns which was responsible in some measure for this change. But the overwhelming masses of all lowland people speak the language of their

European colonizers.[6] The reason for this contrast is that slaves were gathered from diverse parts of Africa and placed individually on different plantations. Unable to communicate with each other in their aboriginal tongues, they quickly came to speak the language of their masters, which in any case they were obliged to learn in order to follow instructions. In the highlands, however, the perpetuation of aboriginal languages was part and parcel of the general tendency to consolidate and emphasize local village patterns. The inability of the Indians to speak Spanish was at the same time, as was their general illiteracy, a convenient re-enforcement of their economic and political subservience.

Another area of clear contrast is that of housing. In the highland region the aboriginal type of dwelling has survived in many communities relatively unaffected by Spanish architectural types. In the lowlands, however, the slaves were brought to live on plantations having a particular type of quarter, set aside for the use of the slaves, with architectural features specifically adapted to the needs of the plantation system.

It should be fairly obvious that there was no need in the plantation areas for the establishment of an African slave hierarchy along the lines of the highland corporate civil-religious system. The political life of the slaves was totally extinguished. The hierarchy of command was from master to overseer to slave, since the slave was essentially the chattel of the owner. The administration of punishment for failure to complete work tasks was directly under the command of the master. Neither the State nor the Church had direct access to the slave population. The master stood between the Church and State and the slaves. This was the reverse of the situation which existed in the highland regions, where the *hacendados* frequently found it necessary to deal with the Church and the State before they were able to make use of Indian labor.

Differential results also obtained in the realm of subsistence. On the plantations the slaves were set to work in a form of agriculture which had existed neither in Africa nor in Europe. Very few African or European subsistence crop techniques were introduced into the lowland regions. Somewhat paradoxically, subsistence agriculture throughout large portions of lowland Latin America is based upon native American Indian crops rather than upon European or African crops. But the fact that maize, beans and manioc were the staples of the plantation areas is easily reconciled with the requirements of the plantation system. The Africans were not brought over as subsistence farmers, nor did there emigrate from Europe any considerable number of homesteading families.

In the highlands, the preservation of the corporate villages, and the establishment of extensive, under-capitalized multi-crop estates, provided the basis for a potentially beneficial amalgam of some of the best features of Old and New World peasant agriculture. Potatoes and corn remained the basic staples, supplemented by wheat, barley and oats. Donkeys and horses replaced llamas as beasts of burden. Oxen were introduced to provide traction for the European plow, which replaced the native foot plow. Most importantly, European domestic animals — sheep, pigs, cows and chickens — became part of the peasant's farmyard population. Quite a different result was achieved in the sugar areas. Some of the most beneficial aspects of the European mixed farming tradition never managed to pass through the plantation filter. Thus in Brazil the *caboclo* farmer continues to practice a form of agriculture which is closer to its Amerindian stone-age predecessors than to the rich and specialized know-how of the Portuguese peasantry. The art of making bread was almost completely lost in the Brazilian interior. Plows gave way to hoes; chickens were tolerated, rather than raised; and milk and cheese never became part of the *caboclo*'s diet. The plantation system also had a debilitating effect upon both European and African arts and crafts. A rich heritage of ceramic craftsmanship, metallurgy and weaving has survived intact in the highland Indian village communities. In the lowland regions, on the other hand, such craft specialties are of a distinctly inferior sort or are totally absent. Much to the dismay of tourists to the lowland regions, the rich folk heritages of craftsmanship in Africa and Europe did not survive the plantation filter.

The effect of the plantations upon the survival of religious elements is of special interest. I would venture to hypothesize that more African religious traits survived in the lowlands than did Indian religious traits in the highlands. This is difficult to substantiate since in both cases there has been a considerable amount of syncretism (blending) of European and aboriginal elements. Moreover, it could always be argued that there was more in common between highland native religions and Catholicism than there was between African religions and Catholicism. Hence, what appears to be purely Catholic in the highlands might in fact actually be partially aboriginal.[7] For example, to what extent does the universal importance of the cross as a talisman actually represent a survival of aboriginal interest in a similar figure associated with the four directions and the sacred Indian number four? From another point of view, however, it is possible to substantiate the claim that African religious survivals are the more vigorous. African religion has survived not in the form of a sprinkling of beliefs in rain gods and dim memories of the ancient religious calendar, but as a number of organic, fully integrated cults, each of which has its own temples, priests, idols and rituals. With few exceptions the comparable phenomena in the highland heritage are associated with periods of rebellion and revitalization movements.[8]

Despite the considerable syncretism which has occurred in the Afro-American cults — variously known as *vodun, candomblé, macumba* — these movements are actually important competitors of formal Catholicism.[9] The fact that African gods are equated with Catholic saints, and that cult members consider themselves to be good Catholics, should not obscure the fundamental opposition between the cults and the Church. Especially threatening to the Catholic hierarchy is the existence of full-time priests and priestesses who are dependent upon cult support for their living. While *shamans* and curers of various degrees of approximation to aboriginal types are quite common in the highlands, their activities are characteristically those of lone individuals, operating without benefit of a supporting organization.

Significantly, these Afro-American cults are not confined to the countryside but are present in almost all of the large Latin American cities in the areas formerly dominated by the slave system. For example, Salvador, the capital of the state of Bahia, is perhaps the most African of all New World cities in the number of its cult centers and in the fidelity with which West African patterns of worship have been maintained. Indeed, recent studies comparing West African Yoruba cults and Bahian Yoruba cults have revealed that the Bahian cults have maintained a high degree of fidelity to the ancestral patterns.

In a typical Bahian cult center ceremonies are held in a special temple, divided into a public dance floor and various sacred rooms accessible only to the priests and cult disciples, who are called the "Daughters of the Saints." Drummers take their place in the public rooms and begin to beat out the rhythms which are believed to be associated with the saints. Under the direction of the Mãe de Santo (the priestess) they emerge from the inner sanctuaries dressed in costumes which reveal their dedication to a particular god. The disciples begin to dance, slowly at first but with greater passion as the tempo increases. If they are fortunate that night, the saint to whom they are dedicated will come down, possess or "ride" them. A sudden paroxysm signals the arrival of the saint. Then the disciples shudder, whirl about and go into a trance. The priestess embraces them, steadies them on their feet, and they remain standing, swaying back and forth until the signal to resume dancing is given. Perfect control and solemnity are maintained despite the fact that the disciples are in a trance deep enough to protect them from pain if they are tested with needles. Lying behind these public performances, there is an intricate and elaborate process whereby novitiates are introduced into the cult centers. Ritual seclusion, sacred paraphernalia, ritual ablution, sacrifice of chickens, sprinkling of novitiates with blood, and many other non-Catholic, or for that matter non-Christian, elements are present.

One cannot escape the conclusion that the remarkable vitality of these African patterns is related to the position of the Catholic Church in the plantation system. In the highlands, the Church dealt directly with the Indian villagers. Throughout the sixteenth and seventeenth centuries, the Church mounted vigorous campaigns to stamp out all vestiges of Indian idolatry. Legally, the highland Indians were exempt from the Inquisition, but in practice the Church maintained a parallel inquisition dedicated to the elimination of heresies exclusively among the Indians. These *visitadores de idolatría* tortured Indians who even deviated to the extent — mild by comparison with the lowland cults — of placing food offerings at mountain shrines.[10]

As we have seen, in considerable measure the success of both the secular and sacred phases of colonialism in the highland regions depended upon the establishment of the fiesta complex and, hence, also upon the eradication of whatever aboriginal patterns had previously existed in the sphere of religion which were incompatible with that complex. Catholicism in the highland regions in other words was a mechanism of control. Religion, however, played no equivalently important role in the control of the slave population or in the integration of the slave system with the larger polity. It will be recalled that the great interest displayed by the Church in Indian affairs was the expression of the possibility of direct Church interference in the lives of the American aboriginals. Slaves, however, had more or less to be written off as far as direct Church control was concerned. The plantation owners did not require the services of the Church for maintaining control over their labor force, nor was there any possibility of the Church's fulfilling its own requirements by imposing economic burdens upon the slaves. From the point of view of the plantation owners, time devoted to fiestas, to the celebration of saint's days, and productive effort allocated for the purposes of supporting the Church hierarchy were totally incompatible with their own self-interest.

Since the African cults prominently feature rhythmic dancing and music and singing in their public phases, it is probable that the plantation owners not only permitted but encouraged these African traits. Certainly, while working in the fields the slaves were permitted to sing and beat out rhythms which maintained the rate of work. In the evening, dancing to the accompaniment of drums was permitted and encouraged as a diversion which helped to maintain the morale of the slaves. As long as the slaves made some pretense of associating the African pantheon with the Catholic pantheon, their masters were not especially dismayed by these heathen performances. It is interesting to note that in the case of the Afro-Bahian cults the predominant rhythm of the public ceremonies is the *samba,* a beat which for the cult members is thus laden with deep religious significance. It is by diffusion out from Afro-American cults that many of the most famous Latin American dance rhythms, shorn of their religious meaning, have entered into the popular music of both North and South America.

It is clear that the plantation system was a powerful instrument of differential cultural growth. As we have seen, it influenced language, art, architecture and political and religious life in a pervasive and lasting fashion. Its differential effect upon race relations, in the narrower sense, was also very great. However, as we shall see in subsequent chapters, this chain of causality with reference to race relations has been obscured and even denied by many respected authorities.

5 / The Brazilian Pattern

The most important feature of Latin American lowland race relations since the abolition of slavery is the absence of sharply defined racial groupings. Unlike both the highlands and the United States, most of the former Latin American slave plantation areas lack racially derived caste-like divisions. The Negroes in the United States and the Indians in highland Latin America may be said to constitute separate social groups. Yet in much of the lowlands of Latin America one is obliged to conclude, as we shall presently see, that there is no such thing as a Negro group or a white group.[1] There are, to be sure, Negroids and Caucasoids, as well as all of the intervening grades resulting from widespread miscegenation, but neither the Negroes nor the mixed or mulatto types nor the whites may be said to constitute by themselves separately identifiable, significant social segments.

A moment's reflection should suffice to bring into prominence the fact that without a method for clearly distinguishing between one group and another, systematic discrimination cannot be practiced. The *sine qua non* of any thoroughgoing minority system is a foolproof method for separating a population into respective superordinate and subordinate groups. In order to prevent the members of a certain group from freely choosing their jobs, voting, enrolling in a school, or joining a club, it is absolutely indispensable that there be a reliable way of knowing who is a member of the group to be segregated and who is a member of the group that is to do the segregating.

Now it just so happens that all of those people in the United States who are certain that they are whites and not Negroes, or vice versa, and all those people in Peru or Ecuador who are certain that they are mestizos and not *Indios,* or vice versa, are whistling through their hats. Genetically speaking, about the only thing any racist can be sure of is that he is a human being. It makes sense to inquire whether a given creature is a man or a chimpanzee, but from the point of view of genetics it is nonsense to ask whether a particular individual is a white *or* a Negro. To be a member of a biological race is to be a member of a population which exhibits a specified frequency of certain kinds of genes. Individuals do not exhibit frequencies of genes; individuals merely have the human complement of genes, a very large but unknown number, most of which are shared in common by all people. When a man says "I am white," all that he can mean scientifically is that he is a member of a population which has been found to have a high frequency of genes for light skin color, thin lips, heavy body hair, medium stature, etc. Since the population of which he is a member is necessarily a hybrid population — actually, all human races are hybrid — there is no way to make certain that *he himself* does not owe a genetic endowment to other populations. This would be the case even if all genotypes were directly expressed in the phenotype. But the fact that a man's actual appearance may be a poor guide to his genetic endowment makes it yet more difficult positively to establish his racial identity. Thus all Caucasoids would be scientifically well-advised to say: "I am probably part Negro," and all Negroes may quite accurately assert: "I am probably part white." The correctness of these statements is assured even if we consider populations which are resident in northern Europe and South Africa, for the archaeological and paleontological evidence quite clearly indicates that there has been gene flow between Europe and Africa for almost a million years. How obviously correct must they be therefore, in such locales as the United States, Latin America and the Republic of South Africa, where known and admitted hybridization has taken place on a vast scale during the past few hundred years! All racial identity, scientifically speaking, is ambiguous. Wherever certainty is expressed on this subject, we can be confident that society has manufactured a social lie in order to help one of its segments take advantage of another.[2]

By what ingenious computation is the genetic tracery of a million years of evolution unraveled and each man assigned his proper social box? In the United States, the mechanism employed is the rule of hypo-descent.[3] This descent rule requires Americans to believe that anyone who is known to have had a Negro ancestor is a Negro. We admit nothing in between. One result of this formula is that millions of us who are genetically more Caucasoid than Negroid are classified as Negroes. "Hypo-descent" means affiliation with the subordinate rather than the superordinate group in order to avoid the ambiguity of intermediate identity. Thus, first-generation children of interracial marriages in the United States are uniformly Negroes, when it is absolutely certain that such children have received half of their hereditary endowment from one parent and half from the other. That a half-white should be a Negro rather than a white cannot be explained by rational argument. The reason for this absurd bit of folk taxonomy is simply that the great blundering machinery of segregation cannot easily adjust itself to degrees of whiteness or darkness. Logically, if there are separate schools for whites and blacks, then there also ought to be separate schools for blonds, brunettes, tans and browns. The rule of hypo-descent is, therefore, an invention which we in the United States have made in order to keep biological facts from intruding into our collective racist fantasies. With it, we have gone so far as to create Alice-in-Wonderland kinds of Negroes about whom people say, "He certainly doesn't look like a Negro." Consider the case of Harry S. Murphy, the young man who recently announced that *he*, rather than James Meredith, had been the first Negro ever to be admitted to the University of Mississippi. Mr. Murphy calls himself a Negro and is apparently regarded as such by those who know his genealogy,[4] and yet he is Caucasoid enough to have spent nine months at "Ole Miss" without attracting the slightest bit of notice. In most parts of lowland Latin America, Mr. Murphy would not only be regarded as white, but he could never "pass" as a Negro.

The contrast between both the United States and high-land patterns and the lowland treatment of racial identity is most dramatically evident in Brazil, although similar contrasts are present everywhere in the former slave, tropical-crop, plantation areas. In Brazil, the whole question of racial identity is resolved in a fashion which is much more befitting the actual complexity of hereditary processes. Racial identity in Brazil is not governed by a rigid descent rule. A Brazilian child is never automatically identified with the racial type of one or both of his parents, nor must his racial type be selected from one of only two possibilities. Over a dozen racial categories may be recognized in conformity with the combinations of hair color, hair texture, eye color and skin color which actually occur. These types grade into each other like the colors of the spectrum and no one category stands significantly isolated from all the rest.

One of the most striking consequences of the Brazilian system of racial identification is that parents and children and even brothers and sisters are frequently accepted as representatives of quite opposite racial types.[5] This feature of the system was confirmed recently by research carried out under the author's supervision in a fishing village in the state of Bahia.[6] A sample of 100 neighbors and relatives were shown photographs of three full sisters and asked to identify the race of each. In only six responses were the three sisters identified by the same racial terms. In all of the remaining cases one or both older sisters were racially distinguished from the baby. Furthermore, there were fourteen respondents who used a different term for all three of the sisters. The most frequent contrast was between *branca* for one and *mulata* or *morena* for one or both of the others, but in a few cases, the range extended over what may have represented the widest contrasts admitted within the respondent's idiosyncratic version of racial types.

It was found, in addition, that a given Brazilian might be called by as many as thirteen different terms by other members of his community. These terms are spread out across practically the entire spectrum of theoretical racial types. A further consequence of the absence of a descent rule is that Brazilians apparently not only disagree about the racial identity of specific individuals, but they also seem to be in disagreement about the abstract meaning of the racial terms as defined by words and phrases. For example, 40 per cent of a representative sample ranked *moreno claro* as a lighter type than *mulato claro*, while 60 per cent reversed this order.

A further note of confusion is introduced by the fact that a given informant was found to be quite capable of employing different racial terms for the same person after a short lapse of time. This phenomenon had previously been predicted by Donald Pierson:

> These and similar terms employed in Brazil are descriptive not only of racial origin but of other and more important phenomena. What is still more significant, their usage *varies with individuals* in keeping with varying personal relationships, and with the same individual at different times in keeping with different moods.[7] [Italics are Pierson's.]

In order systematically to explore the range of terms which might be applied to a given individual a set of nine portrait drawings, variable in hair shade, hair texture, nasal and lip width, and skin tone were also shown to another sample of 100 people. Forty different racial types were now elicited: *branco, preto, sarará, moreno claro, moreno escuro, mulato, moreno, mulato claro, mulato escuro, negro, caboclo, escuro, cabo verde, claro, araçuaba, roxo, amarelo, sarára escuro, côr de canela, preto claro, roxo claro, côr de cinza, vermelho, caboclo escuro, pardo, branco sarará, mambebe, branco caboclado, moreno escuro, mulato sarará, gazula, côr de cinza clara, creolo, louro, moreno claro caboclado, mulato bem claro, branco mulato, roxo de cabelo bom, preto escuro, pelé*. The highest percentage of agreement reached for any of the drawings was 70 per cent *branco* for drawing No. 9. The lowest percentage of agreement was 18 per cent *sarará* for drawing No. 1. Nineteen different terms were elicited by drawing No. 1 and nine different terms were elicited by drawing No. 9.[8] It would seem that if the people of this village ever decided to become segregationists à la Mississippi or Capetown, they would have to build forty different kinds of schools rather than merely two.

A further consequence of the absence of a descent rule in the Brazilian system is that it is possible for people to change their racial identity during their lifetimes. It is known, of course, that a certain number of United States Negroes annually pass into the white group in defiance of our racial rule of descent, and in the highlands, where descent is also important, "passing," as we have seen, occurs quite frequently. In Brazil, however, the changing of "race" does not require the secrecy and the agonizing withdrawal from family and friends which are necessary in this country and among the Indians of the highland regions. In Brazil one can pass to another racial category regardless of how dark one may be without changing one's residence. The passing is accomplished by achieving economic success or high educational status. Brazilians say "Money whitens," meaning that the richer a dark man gets the lighter will be the racial category to which he will be assigned by his friends, relatives and business associates. Similarly, light-skinned individuals who rank extremely low in terms of educational and occupational criteria are frequently regarded as actually being darker in color than they really are. It is this interplay between color and other diagnostics of rank which renders the Brazilian census material on race so dubious.[9] Among the "whites" there are many "brown" persons who because of their superior economic standing are locally classified as "white." On the other hand, among the "blacks," there are many persons who are in reality "brown" but whose extremely low educational and occupational status displaces them into the "black" category.

This means in effect that there are no subjectively meaningful Brazilian social groups based exclusively upon racial criteria. The terms Negro *(preto)* and white *(branco)* could denote clear-cut population segments for nobody but a physical anthropologist. In the actual dynamics of everyday life, superordinate-subordinate relationships are determined by the interplay between a variety of achieved and ascribed statuses, of which race is an important but not decisive element. It is evident that in the Northeast of Brazil the fact that an individual manifests a particular set of physical characteristics does not by itself determine a single status-role.[10]

The lack of a descent rule, the high frequency of "passing," marked semantic ambiguity of both an abstract and referential sort, and the complicated interplay between physical appearance and other diagnostics or rank were in the initial phases of research in northeastern Brazil confused with an absence of racial prejudice. Blanket statements asserting that "Brazil has no racial prejudice" became popular among Brazilian diplomats and other official and semi-official spokesmen who shared Gilberto Freyre's belief that:

> With respect to race relations, the Brazilian situation is probably the nearest approach to paradise to be found anywhere in the world.[11]

Even Donald Pierson, the first North American to make a detailed study of Brazilian race relations, was somewhat carried away by his enthusiasm for Bahian inter-racial democracy, and tended to underestimate the amount of racial prejudice which actually existed, and which every Brazilian knows full well exists, except when talking to United States citizens.

Additional studies have since documented the prevalence of stereotypes against "Negroes" and Negroid physical features.[12] Most Brazilians abstractly regard Negroes as innately inferior in intelligence, honesty and dependability. Negroid physical features are universally (even by "Negroes" themselves) believed to be less desirable and less beautiful than Caucasoid features. In most of their evaluations of the Negro as an abstract type, the whites are inclined to deride and slander. Prejudiced and stereotyped opinions about people of intermediate physical appearance are also common. On the whole, there is an ideal racial ranking gradient, in which whites occupy the favorable extreme, Negroes the unfavorable extreme and mulattoes the various intermediate positions.[13]

But these ideological phenomena do not seriously affect actual behavior. What people say they will or will not do with respect to *pretos* and *mulatos* does not issue into actual behavior. Indeed, extremely prejudiced Brazilians have been observed to behave with marked deference toward representatives of the very types whom they allege to be most inferior. Racial prejudice in Brazil, in other words, is not accompanied by systematic racial segregation and discrimination. The reason for this paradox should be clear: Despite the "ideal" stereotypes, there is no "actual" status-role for the Negro as a Negro, for the white as a white, or for the *mulato* as a *mulato*. There are no racial groups.[14] Before two individuals can decide how they ought to behave toward each other they must know more than merely that one is dark-skinned and the other light. A Brazilian is never merely a "white man" or a "colored man"; he is a rich, well educated white man or a poor, uneducated white man; a rich, well educated colored man or a poor, uneducated colored man. The outcome of this qualification of race by education and economics determines one's class identity. It is one's class and not one's race which determines the adoption of subordinate and superordinate attitudes between specific individuals in face-to-face relations. It is class which determines who will be admitted to hotels, restaurants and social clubs; who will get preferential treatment in stores, churches, night clubs and travel accommodations; and who will have the best chance among a group of marriage suitors. There are no racial groups against which discrimination occurs. Instead, there are class groups. Color is one of the criteria of class identity; but it is not the only criterion.

Brazil's classes, unlike those of the United States, tend to include a very wide variety of racial types. Also, unlike those of the United States, the disabilities of class membership are immensely more severe and unshakable. Thus, while it is true that racial prejudice exerts only a negligible influence in establishing an individual's class membership, this membership is less mutable, and immensely more significant for everyday relationships and long-range life expectations, than is the case in our own culture. Race discrimination is per se mild and equivocal; class discrimination, however, produces disabilities and inequalities of a sharp, persistent and pervasive sort. I have elsewhere argued that it is not Brazil's color groups, but her classes which correspond most closely to the Indians in highland Latin America and to the Negroes in the United States.

This class discrimination has recently been summarized by Thales de Azevedo for Bahian society. Dr. Azevedo regards the Bahian social hierarchy as consisting of three classes, with the most important social cleavage between the middle and lower groups. These two groups are popularly perceived as *os ricos* and *os pobres*, the rich and the poor. The rich are sometimes called the whites. They are those who don't work hard, those who work with their heads or those who wear a tie, the *doutores*, the people with college-level degrees, the government workers, the powerful businessmen. The poor are sometimes called the Negroes. "They are those who sweat. They are the humble ones."

Of crucial significance here is the fact that despite the equation of the rich with whites and of the poor with Negroes, the actual facts of the matter are that both groups are racially mixed. Negroes occur, although in small percentages, among the "whites" as well as among the "Negroes." And whites occur, again with smaller percentages but nonetheless in significant numbers, among the so-called *pobres* or "Negroes."

These racially mixed groups confront each other in a manner which is strikingly reminiscent of the accommodations which exist between the supposedly racially homogeneous minority groups in the United States. Thus, as Azevedo points out, the people of the lower group are obliged to address the superior group with the title *Dona* for women and *O senhor* for men. The "inferior" person is careful not to use *você* to address members of the superior group. Kissing among women; the intimate goodbye signal made with the fingers; and the handshake and *abraço* (embrace) are rarely employed in asymmetrical relationships. If a superior shakes hands with an inferior, the latter must let the superior take his hand without responding with a clasp of his own.

Other mechanisms regulate the spatial positions and limit the use of intimate gestures and words. A member of the inferior group is received into the house of an upper- or middle-class person but rarely does he seat himself in the living room or at the dinner table. If a meal is offered to him, he eats in the kitchen, in the pantry, or even at the table but separated, either before or after the others. Marriages rarely cross the lines which separate these two groups. The clothing is different. The educational system is structured in relationship to the two groups. Public schools are attended practically exclusively by the *pobres* and private schools only by the members of the superior group. A *pobre* caught at a crime by a policeman is taken to a comfortless prison where he may be treated brutally and where his companions are criminals, bums, alcoholics and beggars. The individual of the higher group in the same circumstances almost always finds a way to avoid immediate imprisonment. If he is taken prisoner, he is brought to the police station discreetly in an automobile. He may be taken to the hospital rather than to prison, while persons with degrees are *legally* entitled to be put in special prisons.

This description of the differential privileges of the "rich" and the "poor" in Brazil could be expanded to much greater lengths. Class "discrimination" operates in hotels, hospitals, restaurants, night clubs, housing and many other public and semi-public institutions. Of course, a good deal of this "discrimination" automatically results merely from the inability of some individuals to pay for certain goods and services. Such discrimination is a part of any system where goods and services are bought and sold and where there are pecuniary inequalities. But in northeastern Brazil, the pecuniary inequalities are so great that a large segment of the population is unable to purchase the quantities and qualities of goods and services which are deemed the minimum prerequisite for a comfortable existence by those who provide the model for the "good life." The Brazilian masses are not only unable to buy servants, yachts, country estates, *pâté de foie gras* and trips around the world (some annoying results of pecuniary "discrimination" in the United States), but bread and meat, a suit of clothes, shoes, adequate medical care, beds, high-school education, comfortable transport and many other items which are deemed minimum essentials in advanced industrial societies. Under such conditions, the issue of racial discrimination is scarcely a vital one. Lower-class whites and lower-class colored people are alike segregated and "discriminated" against, one perhaps slightly more than the other; but where the common deprivations are so pervasive, where upward mobility is so restricted, all of the familiar symptoms of racial discrimination tend to be subsumed by the class differentials.

Thus, although the pattern of "race" relations in Brazil contrasts markedly with that of the United States, especially with that of the South, once Brazil's lower class is accorded its proper structural significance as the equivalent of the "Negroes" in the United States, the stratification systems of the two countries actually bear a very close resemblance to each other. In both cases, the fundamental heritage of the slave plantation was the creation of severely handicapped minorities, darker in color than the rest of the population. Let those who regard Brazil as a "racial paradise" remember that this paradise is occupied only by fictional creatures. The real men and women of Bahia are not members of "races," except insofar as any collection of human beings may be said to have an objective racial identity. As far as actual behavior is concerned, "races" do not exist for the Brazilians. But classes exist both for the observer and *for* the Brazilians. This is the first fact to be digested if one is curious about why racial identity per se is a mild and wavering thing in Brazil, while in the United States, it is for millions of people a passport to hell.

6 / The Myth of the Friendly Master

The argument in the previous chapters has been that differences in race relations within Latin America are at root a matter of the labor systems in which the respective subordinate and superordinate groups became enmeshed. I have already attempted to show how a number of cultural traits and institutions which were permitted to survive, or were deliberately encouraged under one system, were discouraged or suppressed in the other. It remains to be shown how the specific combination of features which characterize lowland race relations more narrowly construed can be accounted for by the same set of principles.

At present, probably the majority of American scholars who have found a moment to ponder the peculiar aspects of the Brazilian interracial "paradise" are devoted to an opposite belief. What could be more obvious than the inadequacy of a materialist explanation of the Brazilian pattern? How can plantation slavery be made to explain anything about the lack of interracial hostility in Brazil? Was it not a plantation system in the United States South which bred a condition contrary in every detail to that of Brazil?

The current vogue of opinion about this contrast derives in large measure from the work of Frank Tannenbaum, a noted United States historian, and Gilberto Freyre, Brazil's best known sociologist. The theories of these influential scholars overlap at many points. It is their contention that the laws, values, religious precepts and personalities of the English colonists differed from those of the Iberian colonists.

These initial psychological and ideological differences were sufficient to overcome whatever tendency the plantation system may have exerted toward parallel rather than divergent evolution.

Freyre's theories, originally proposed in his classic study of Brazilian plantation life, *Casa grande e senzala*, have remained virtually unchanged for over thirty years. What most impresses Freyre about Brazilian slavery is the alleged easy-going, humanized relations between master and slave, especially between master and female slave. Slaves, while subject to certain disabilities and although sometimes cruelly treated, frequently came to play an emotionally significant role in the intimate life of their white owners. A high rate of miscegenation was one of the hallmarks of this empathy between the races. The Portuguese not only took Negro and mulatto women as mistresses and concubines, but they sometimes spurned their white wives in order to enjoy the favors of duskier beauties. Behind these favorable omens, visible from the very first days of contact, was a fundamental fact of national character, namely, the Portuguese had no color prejudice. On the contrary, their long experience under Moorish tutelage is said to have prepared them to regard people of darker hue as equals, if not superiors:

> The singular predisposition of the Portuguese to the hybrid, slave-exploiting colonization of the tropics is to be explained in large part by the ethnic or, better, the cultural past of a people existing indeterminately between Europe and Africa and belonging uncompromisingly to neither one nor the other of the two continents.[1]

Other colonizers were not as successful as the Portuguese because their libidos were more conservative. Especially poorly endowed sexually were the "Anglo-Saxon Protestants."

> The truth is that in Brazil, contrary to what is to be observed in other American countries and in those parts of Africa that have been recently colonized by Europeans, the primitive culture — the Amerindian as well as the African — has not been isolated into hard, dry indigestible lumps...Neither did the social

relations between the two races, the conquering and the indigenous one, ever reach that point of sharp antipathy or hatred, the grating sound of which reaches our ears from all the countries that have been colonized by Anglo-Saxon Protestants. The friction here (in Brazil) was smoothed by the lubricating oil of a deep-going miscegenation . . .[2]

The next and fatal step in this line of reasoning is to assert that the special psychological equipment of the Portuguese, not only in Brazil but everywhere in "The World the Portuguese Created,"[3] yields hybrids and interracial harmony. In 1952, after a tour of Portuguese colonies as an honored guest of the Salazar government, Freyre declared that the Portuguese were surrounded in the Orient, America and Africa with half-caste "luso-populations" and "a sympathy on the part of the native which contrasts with the veiled or open hatred directed toward the other Europeans."[4]

How Freyre could have been hoodwinked into finding resemblances between race relations in Angola and Mozambique and Brazil is hard to imagine. My own findings, based on a year of field work in Mozambique, have since been supported by the field and library research of James Duffy.[5] If any reasonable doubts remained about the falsity of Freyre's luso-tropical theory, tragic events in Angola should by now have swept them away. The fact is that the Portuguese are responsible for setting off the bloodiest of all of the recent engagements between whites and Negroes in Africa (including the Mau Mau). And the Portuguese, alone of all the former African colonial powers, now stand shoulder to shoulder with the citizens of that incorrigible citadel of white supremacy, the Repubic of South Africa, baited and damned from Zanzibar to Lagos.

It is true that the Portuguese *in Portugal* tend to be rather neutral on the subject of color differences, if they ever think about such things at all. But this datum can only be significant to those who believe that discrimination is caused by prejudice, when the true relationship is quite the opposite. When the innocent Portuguese emigrants get to Africa, they find that legally, economically and socially, white men can take advantage of black men, and it doesn't take long for them to join in the act. Within a year after his arrival, the Portuguese learns that blacks are inferior to whites, that the Africans have to be kept in their place, and that they are indolent by nature and have to be forced to work. What we call prejudices are merely the rationalizations which we acquire in order to prove to ourselves that the human beings whom we harm are not worthy of better treatment.

Actually the whole issue of the alleged lack of racial or color prejudice among the Portuguese (and by extension among the Spanish as well) is totally irrelevant to the main question. If, as asserted, the Iberians initially lacked any color prejudice, what light does this shed upon the Brazilian and other Latin American lowland interracial systems? The distinguishing feature of these systems is not that whites have no color prejudices. On the contrary, color prejudice as we have seen is a conspicuous and regular feature in all the plantation areas. The parts of the system which need explaining are the absence of a descent rule; the absence of distinct socially significant racial groups; and the ambiguity of racial identity. In Portuguese Africa none of these features are present. The state rules on who is a native and who is a white and the condition of being a native is hereditary:

Individuals of the Negro race or their descendants who were born or habitually reside in the said Provinces and who do not yet possess the learning and the social and individual habits presupposed for the integral application of the public and private law of Portuguese citizens are considered to be 'natives.'[6]

As for miscegenation, the supposedly color-blind Portuguese libido had managed by 1950 to produce slightly more than 50,000 officially recognized mixed types in an African population of 10 million after 400 years of contact.[7] This record should be compared with the product of the monochromatic libidos of the Dutch invaders of South Africa—in Freyre's terms Anglo-Saxon Protestants to the hilt—a million and a half official hybrids (coloureds).[8] It is time that grown men stopped talking about racially prejudiced sexuality. In general, when human beings have the power, the opportunity and the need, they will mate with members of the opposite sex regardless of color or the identity of grandfather. Whenever free breeding in a human population is restricted, it is because a larger system of social relations is menaced by such freedom.

This is one of the points about which Tannenbaum and Freyre disagree. Tannenbaum quite correctly observes that "the process of miscegenation was part of the system of slavery, and not just of Brazilian slavery. . . . The dynamics of race contact and sex interests were stronger than prejudice. . . . This same mingling of the races and classes occurred in the United States. The record is replete with the occurrence, in spite of law, doctrine, and belief. Every traveler in the South before the Civil War comments on the widespread miscegenation. . . ."[9] But it should also be pointed out that there is no concrete evidence to indicate that the rank and file of English colonists were initially any more or less prejudiced than the Latins. It is true that the English colonists very early enacted laws intended to prevent marriage between white women and Negro men and between white men and Negro women. Far from indicating a heritage of anti-Negro prejudices, however, these laws confirm the presence of strong attraction between the males and females of both races. The need for legal restriction certainly suggests that miscegenation was not at all odious to many of the English colonists.

The idea of assigning differential statuses to white indentured servants and Negro workers was definitely not a significant part of the ideological baggage brought over by the earliest colonists, at least not to an extent demonstrably greater than among the Latin colonists. It is true, as Carl Degler has shown, that the differentiation between white indentured servants and Negro indentured servants had become conspicuous before the middle of the seventeenth century even though the legal formulation was not completed until the end of the century. But who would want to suggest that there was absolutely no prejudice against the Negroes immediately after contact? Ethnocentrism is a universal feature of inter-group relations and obviously both the English and the Iberians were prejudiced against foreigners, white and black. The facts of life in the New World were such, however, that Negroes, being the most defenseless of all the immigrant groups, were discriminated against and exploited more than any others. Thus the Negroes were not enslaved because the British colonists specifically despised dark-skinned people and regarded them alone as properly suited to slavery; the Negroes came to be the object of the virulent prejudices because they and they alone could be enslaved. Judging from the very nasty treatment suffered by white indentured servants, it was obviously not sentiment which prevented the Virginia planters from enslaving their fellow Englishmen. They undoubtedly would have done so had they been able to get away with it. But such a policy was out of the question as long as there was a King and a Parliament in England.

The absence of preconceived notions about what ought to be the treatment of enslaved peoples forms a central theme in Tannenbaum's explanation of United States race relations. According to Tannenbaum, since the English had gotten rid of slavery long before the Discovery, they had no body of laws or traditions which regulated and humanized the slave status. Why this legal lacuna should have been significant for the course run by slavery in the United States is quite obscure. Even Degler, who accepts the Freyre-Tannenbaum approach, points out that it was "possible for almost any kind of status to be worked out."[10] One might reasonably conclude that the first settlers were not overly concerned with race differences, and that they might have remained that way (as many Englishmen have) had they not been brought into contact with Negroes under conditions wholly dictated by the implacable demands of a noxious and "peculiar" institution.

Let us turn now to the main substance of Tannenbaum's theory. Tannenbaum correctly believes that the critical difference between race relations in the United States and in Latin America resides in the physical and psychological (he says "moral") separation of the Negro from the rest of society. "In spite of his adaptability, his willingness, and his competence, in spite of his complete identification with the *mores* of the United States, he is excluded and denied. . . ." Also, quite correctly, Tannenbaum stresses the critical role of the free Negro and mulatto in Latin America. Manumission appears to have been much more common, and the position of the freed man was much more secure than elsewhere.

Free Negroes and mulattoes quickly came to outnumber the slaves. However, according to Tannenbaum, this phenomenon came about because the slave was endowed with "a moral personality before emancipation ... which ... made the transition from slavery to freedom easy and his incorporation into the free community natural."[11] The Negro and mulatto were never sharply cut off from the rest of society because the Latin slave was never cut off from the rest of humanity. This was because slavery in southern Europe and Latin America was embedded in a legal, ethical, moral and religious matrix which conspired to preserve the slave's individual integrity as the possessor of an immortal human soul. The "definition" of the slave as merely an unfortunate human being, primarily according to state and canonical code, is given most weight:

> For if one thing stands out clearly from the study of slavery, it is that the definition of man as a moral being proved the most important influence both in the treatment of the slave and in the final abolition of slavery.[12]

Note that it is not merely being claimed that there was a critical difference between Latin American and United States race relations during and after slavery, but that the very institution of slavery itself was one thing in the United States and the British West Indies and another thing in Latin America:

> There were briefly speaking, three slave systems in the Western Hemisphere. The British, American, Dutch, and Danish were at one extreme, and the Spanish and Portuguese at the other. In between these two fell the French. ... If one were forced to arrange these systems of slavery in order of severity, the Dutch would seem to stand as the harshest, the Portuguese as the mildest, and the French in between. ...[13]

The contention that the condition of the average slave in the English colonies was worse than that of the average slave in the Latin colonies obscures the main task which confronts us, which is to explain why the treatment of the free mulatto and free Negro were and are so different. To try to explain why the slaves were treated better in Latin

America than in the United States is a waste of time, for there is no conceivable way in which we can now be certain that they were indeed treated better in one place than the other. It is true that a large number of travelers can be cited, especially from the nineteenth century, who were convinced that the slaves were happier under Spanish and Portuguese masters than under United States masters. But there was plenty of dissenting opinion. Tannenbaum makes no provision for the fact that the English planters had what we would today call a very bad press, since thousands of intellectuals among their own countrymen were in the vanguard of the abolitionist movement. The West Indian and Southern planters, of course, were in total disagreement with those who preferred slavery under foreign masters. Actually all of the distinctions between the Anglo-American and Latin slave systems which Tannenbaum proposes were already the subject of debate at the beginning of the eighteenth century between Anglo-American abolitionists and Anglo-American planters. For example, in 1827, the Jamaican planter Alexander Barclay responded to the English critics of his island's slave system as follows:

> According to Mr. Stephen [author of *Slavery of the British West India Colonies*] there exists among his countrymen in the West Indies, an universal feeling of hatred and contempt of the Negroes.... It is by this assumed hatred and contempt, that he strives to give probability to the most incredible charges of cruelty and oppression; and indeed, in many cases, this alleged feeling of aversion and abhorrence on the part of the whites, is the sole ground for supposing that the charges should be made, and the sole proof of them. Such things must have happened, because the colonists hate the Negroes. Now, I most solemnly affirm, not only that I am unconscious of any such surely unnatural feelings having place in my own breast, but that I have never seen proof of its existence in the breasts of others.[14]

All slave-owners of whatever nationality always seem to have been convinced that "their" slaves were the happiest of earthly beings. Barclay claims that the Jamaican slaves celebrated the cane harvest with an inter-racial dance:

In the evening, they assemble in their master's or manager's house, and, as a matter of course, take possession of the largest room, bringing with them a fiddle and tambourine. Here all authority and all distinction of colour ceases; black and white, overseer and book-keeper, mingle together in the dance.[15]

At Christmas time the same thing happens. The slaves

... proceed to the neighbouring plantation villages, and always visit the master's or manager's house, into which they enter without ceremony, and where they are joined by the white people in a dance.[16]

Concludes Barclay:

All is life and joy, and certainly it is one of the most pleasing sights that can be imagined.[17]

In the United States, equally rapturous descriptions of the slave's lot were a conspicuous part of the ideological war between North and South. Many planters felt that their slaves were better off than the mass of Northern whites, and Southern poets did not hesitate to cap their comparisons of free and slave labor with panegyrics

... on the happy life of the slave, with all his needs provided, working happily in the fields by day, enjoying the warm society of his family in the cabin at night, idling through life in "the summer shade, the winter sun," and without fear of the poorhouse at its close ... until we finally find the slave "luxuriating" in a "lotus-bearing paradise."[18]

If one were so inclined by lack of an understanding of the nature of sociological evidence, it would not be difficult to paint a picture in which the position of the Anglo-American slave system was promoted from last to first place. Freyre himself provides enough material on cruelty in the Brazilian plantations to fill at least a corner in a chamber of horrors:

And how, in truth, are the hearts of us Brazilians to acquire the social virtues if from the moment we open our eyes we see about us the cruel distinction between master and slave, and behold the former, at the slightest provocation or sometimes out of mere whim, mercilessly rending the flesh of our own kind with lashes?[19]

There are not two or three but many instances

of the cruelties of the ladies of the big house toward
their helpless blacks. There are tales of *sinhámoças*
who had the eyes of pretty *mucamas* gouged out and
then had them served to their husband for dessert,
in a jelly-dish, floating in blood that was still fresh. . . .
There were others who kicked out the teeth of their
women slaves with their boots, or who had their
breasts cut off, their nails drawn, or their faces and
ears burned.[20]

Another Brazilian observer, Arthur Ramos, goes even
further:

During the period, of slavery, suppression and
punishment prevented almost any spontaneous activity.
. . . The number of instruments of torture employed
was numerous and profoundly odious. . . . There was
the *tronco,* of wood or of iron, an instrument which
held the slave fast at the ankles and in the grip of
which he was often kept for days on end; the *libambo*
which gripped the unfortunate victim fast at the neck;
the *algemas* and the *anjinhos,* which held the hands
tightly, crushing the thumbs. . . . Some plantation
owners of more perverted inclinations used the so-
called *novenas* and *trezenas.* . . . The Negroes tied face
down on the ground, were beaten with the rawhide
whip on from nine to thirteen consecutive nights. . . .[21]

The testimony of the travelers, poets, planters, abolitionists and scholars in this matter, however, is worthless.
Better to dispute the number of angels on a pinhead than to
argue that one country's slavery is superior to another's. The
slaves, wherever they were, didn't like it; they killed themselves and they killed their masters; over and over again
they risked being torn apart by hounds and the most despic-
able tortures in order to escape the life to which they were
condemned. It is a well known fact that Brazil was second to
none in the number of its fugitive slaves and its slave revolts.
In the seventeenth century one successful group held out in
the famous *quilombo* of Palmares for sixty-seven years and
in the nineteenth century scarcely a year went by without an
actual or intended revolt.[22]

In a recent book, the historian Stanley M. Elkins attempts to save Tannenbaum's theory by admitting that slavery

in the United States (at least by 1850) "in a 'physical' sense was in general, probably, quite mild" and that there were very "severe" sides to the Spanish and Portuguese systems.[23] Elkins assures us, however, that even if slavery had been milder here than anywhere else in the Western Hemisphere, "it would still be missing the point to make the comparison in terms of physical comfort. In one case we would be dealing with cruelty of man to man, and, in the other, with the care, maintenance, and indulgence of men toward creatures who were legally and morally *not* men—not in the sense that Christendom had traditionally defined man's nature."[24] It is devoutly to be hoped that Elkins shall never be able to test his exquisite sense of equity by experiencing first thirty lashes dealt out by someone who calls him a black man and then a second thirty from someone who calls him a black devil. But if there be such talents as Elkins' among us, we had better take a closer look at the proposition that the Negro was regarded as a human being by the Latin colonists but not by the Anglo-Saxons. The principal source of evidence for this resides in the law codes by which the respective slave systems were theoretically regulated. Admittedly, these codes do show a considerable difference of legal opinion as to the definition of a slave. The Spanish and Portuguese codes were essentially continuations of medieval regulations stretching back ultimately to Roman law. The British and American colonial codes were the original creations of the New World planter class, developed first in the West Indies (Barbados) and then copied throughout the South.[25] Although the Constitution of the United States said that slaves were persons, state laws said they were chattels—mere property. "Slave-holders, legislators, and judges were forever trying to make property out of them ... They simply did not regard them as human beings."[26] On the other hand, Spanish and Portuguese slave laws did, as Tannenbaum claims, specifically preserve the human identity of the slave: "The distinction between slavery and freedom is a product of accident and misfortune, and the free man might have been a slave."[27] From this there flowed a number of rights, of which Fernando Ortiz identifies four as most significant: (1) the right to marry freely; (2) the right to seek out another master if any were too

severe; (3) the right of owning property; and (4) the right
to buy freedom.[28] Tannenbaum shows how all of the U. S.
slave states denied these rights. He goes further and shows
how the U. S. slaves were virtually left without legal remedy
for harms committed upon them, and he emphasizes the casual fines which protected the life of a slave under the early
laws,[29] and the total lack of legal recognition given to the
slave's affinal or consanguine family. Indeed, for every favorable section in the Spanish law, both Elkins and Tannenbaum
readily find an unfavorable section in the Anglo-Saxon codes.

What the laws of the Spanish and Portuguese kings had
to do with the attitudes and values of the Spanish and Portuguese planters, however, baffles one's imagination. The
Crown could publish all the laws it wanted, but in the lowlands, sugar was king. If there were any Portuguese or
Spanish planters who were aware of their legal obligations
toward the slaves, it would require systematic misread-
ing of colonialism, past and present, to suppose that these
laws psychologically represented anything more than the
flatus of a pack of ill-informed Colonel Blimps who didn't
even know what a proper cane field looked like. Ortiz leaves
no room for doubt in the case of Cuba. Yes, the slave had legal
rights, "But these rights were not viable . . . if they contrast
with the barbaric laws of the French and above all, of the
English colonies, it was no less certain that all of these rights
were illusory, especially in earlier times. . . ." Sanctity of the
family? "Man and wife were permanently separated, sold in
separate places, and separated from their children."[30] "How
many times was a son sold by his father!" and "Pregnant or
nursing slaves were sold with or without their actual or fu-
ture offspring."[31] Protection of the law? "The sugar and coffee plantations were in fact feudal domains where the only
authority recognized was that of the master. . . . Could the
Negroes hope in these circumstances to change masters? The
rawhide would quiet their voices. . . ." Rights to property?
"From what I have said in relation to the work of the rural
slave, to speak of his right to hold property and to buy freedom, is futile. . . ." "But I repeat, the plantation slave was
treated like a beast, like a being to whom human character
was denied. . . ."[32]

Tannenbaum makes much of the fact that there was no set of ancient slave laws to which the Anglo-Saxon planters or the slaves could turn for guidance. He prominently displays the meager penalties attached to murder of slaves as examples of their sub-human status in the eyes of the Anglo-Saxon colonists. But Ortiz informs us that "it was not until 1842 that there was any specific legal regulation of the form of punishment which a Cuban master could give his slave."[33] Actually it turns out that "the state did not concern itself with the limitation of the arbitrary power of the master in relation to the punishment of his slave until after the abolition of slavery [1880]."[34]

In Brazil, as everywhere in the colonial world, law and reality bore an equally small resemblance to each other. Stanley Stein's recent historical study of slavery in the county of Vassouras during the last century yields a picture almost totally at variance with that drawn by Gilberto Freyre for the earlier plantations. The Vassouras planters went about their business, methodically buying, working, beating and selling their slaves, in whatever fashion yielded the most coffee with the least expense. The master's will was supreme. "It was difficult to apply legal restraints to the planter's use of the lash."[35]

Typical is an eyewitness account of a beating told by an ex-slave. On order from the master, two drivers bound and beat a slave while the slave folk stood in line, free folk watching from further back. The slave died that night and his corpse, dumped into a wicker basket, was borne by night to the slave cemetery of the plantation and dropped into a hastily dug grave. *"Slaves could not complain to the police, only another fazendeiro* [master] *could do that,"* explained the eyewitness.[36] [Italics are mine.]

If Stein's picture of nineteenth-century Vassouras is accurate —and it is the most carefully documented study of its kind in existence—then the following recent pronouncement from Charles Boxer will have to be accepted minus the time restriction:

The common belief that the Brazilian was an exceptionally kind master is applicable only to the 19th century under the Empire, and it is contradicted for the colonial period by the testimony of numerous reliable eyewitnesses from Vieira to Vilhena, to say nothing of the official correspondence between the colonial authorities and the Crown.[37]

Of special interest in Boxer's refutation of the myth of the friendly master is the evidence which shows that Brazilian planters and miners did not accept the legal decisions which awarded human souls and human personalities to the slaves. The Brazilian slave owners were convinced that Negroes were descended from Cain, black and "therefore not people like ourselves." Making due allowance for exceptions and the special circumstances of household slaves, Boxer concludes that "it remains true that by and large colonial Brazil was indeed a 'hell for blacks.' "[38]

7 / The Origin of the
Descent Rule

At one point, and one point only, is there a demonstrable correlation between the laws and behavior, the ideal and the actual, in Tannenbaum's theory: the Spanish and Portuguese codes ideally drew no distinction between the ex-slave and the citizen, and actual behavior followed suit. The large hybrid populations of Latin America were not discriminated against *solely* because they were descended from slaves; it is definitely verifiable that all hybrids were not and are not forced back into a sharply separated Negro group by application of a rule of descent. This was true during slavery and it was true after slavery. With abolition, because a continuous color spectrum of free men had already existed for at least 200 years, ex-slaves and descendants of slaves were not pitted against whites in the bitter struggle which marks the career of our own Jim Crow.

However, to argue that it was the Spanish and Portuguese slave codes and slave traditions which gave rise to these real and substantial differences in the treatment of the free Negro and mulatto is to miss the essential point about the evolution of the New World plantation systems. If traditional laws and values were alone necessary to get the planters to manumit their slaves, and treat free colored people like human beings, the precedents among the English colonists were surely greater than among the Latins.

If anything, the laws and traditions of England conspired to make its colonists abhor anything that smacked of slavery. And so it was in England that in 1705 Chief Justice

Holt could say, "As soon as a Negro comes into England he becomes free."[1] Let it not be forgotten that five of the original thirteen states — New Hampshire, Massachusetts, Connecticut, Rhode Island and Pennsylvania, plus the independent state of Vermont — began programs of complete emancipation before the federal Constitutional Convention met in 1787. Partial anti-slavery measures were enacted by New York in 1788, and total emancipation in 1799, while New Jersey began to pass anti-slavery legislation in 1786.[2] Furthermore, all of the original states which abolished slavery lived up to the declared principles of the Declaration of Independence and the Constitution to a remarkable degree in their treatment of emancipated slaves. "They were citizens of their respective states the same as were Negroes who were free at the time of independence."[3]

There were no restrictions prior to 1800 upon Negroes voting in any state which had abolished slavery. They were voting at that time and continued to vote without interruption in New Hampshire, Vermont, Rhode Island, and the two slave states of New York and New Jersey.

It was only later that Connecticut (1814) and Pennsylvania (1837) got around to imposing restrictions. Although the slave codes of New York, New Jersey and Pennsylvania had forbidden slaves to testify in court cases involving white persons, these laws were never applied to free Negroes, and "there were no such laws in New England. . . . Nor were there any distinctions whatever in criminal law, judicial procedure, and punishments." In all of the Northern states, therefore, Negroes were citizens "by enjoyment of full political equality, by lack of any statements to the contrary in any constitution or law, by complete absence of legal distinction based on color, and by specific legal and constitutional declaration. . . ."[4]

We see, therefore, that if past laws and values had a significant role to play in the treatment of Negroes and mulattoes, the hounding persecution of the free Negroes and mulattoes should never have occurred in the English colonies. For contrary to the oft-repeated assertion that there was no matrix of English law or tradition into which the slave could fit, it is quite obvious that very specific laws and traditions existed to guide the Anglo-Saxon colonists. These laws and traditions held that all men had natural rights, that the Negroes were men and that slaves ought to become citizens. That the Constitution asserts "all men are created equal" is not some monstrous hypocrisy perpetrated by the founding fathers. It was an expression of a general Northern and enlightened Southern belief that slavery was an institution which was incompatible with the laws and traditions of civilized Englishmen. That the American versions of these laws were later subverted by court decisions and that the Constitution's guarantee of freedom and equality became a grim joke is surely ample testimony to the futility of trying to understand socio-cultural evolution in terms of such factors.

Understanding of the differences in the status of free "non-whites" in the plantation world can only emerge when one forthrightly inquires why a system which blurred the distinction between Negro and white was materially advantageous to one set of planters, while it was the opposite to another. One can be certain that if it had been materially disadvantageous to the Latin colonists, it would never have been tolerated — Romans, *Siete Partidas* and the Catholic Church notwithstanding. For one thing is clear, the slavocracy in both the Latin and Anglo-Saxon colonies held the whip hand not only over the slaves but over the agents of civil and ecclesiastical authority. To make second-class citizens out of all descendants of slaves was surely no greater task, given sufficient material reason, than to make slaves out of men and brutes out of slaves.

Although the slave plantation per se was remarkably similar in its effects regardless of the cultural background of the slaves or slave-owners,[5] the natural, demographic and institutional environment with which slavery articulated and interacted was by no means uniform. It is the obligation of all those who wish to explain the difference between United States and Latin American race relations to examine these material conditions first, before concluding that it was the mystique of the Portuguese or Spanish soul that made the difference.

The first important consideration is demographic. Latin America and the United States experienced totally different patterns of settlement. When Spain and Portugal began their occupation of the New World, they were harassed by severe domestic manpower shortages, which made it extremely difficult for them to find colonists for their far-flung empires. Furthermore, in the New World the conditions under which such colonists were to settle were themselves antithetical to large-scale emigration. In the highlands a dense aboriginal population was already utilizing most of the arable land under the tutelage of the *encomenderos* and *hacendados*. In the lowlands large-scale emigration, supposing there had been a sufficient number of potential settlers, was obstructed by the monopolization of the best coastal lands by the slave-owning sugar planters. Only a handful of Portuguese migrated to Brazil during the sixteenth century. In the seventeenth century, a deliberate policy of *restricting* emigration to Brazil was pursued, out of fear that Portugal was being depopulated. Cried the Jesuit father Antonio Vieira, "Where are our men? Upon every alarm in Alentejo it is necessary to take students from the university, tradesmen from their shops, laborers from the plough!"[6]

The migrations of Englishmen and Britishers to the New World followed an entirely different rhythm. Although the movement began almost a century later, it quickly achieved a magnitude that was to have no parallel in Latin America until the end of the nineteenth century. Between 1509 and 1790 only 150,000 people emigrated from Spain to the entire New World, but between 1600 and 1700, 500,000 English and Britishers moved to the North American territories.

The reason for this accelerated rate of migration is not hard to find:

As opposed to Spain and Portugal, harassed by a permanent manpower scarcity when starting to occupy the Western Hemisphere, seventeenth-century England had an abundant population surplus, owing to the far-reaching changes affecting the country's agriculture since the previous century.[7]

The changes in question were the enclosures by which

much of England's farming population was being forced off the land in order to make way for sheep-raising (in turn stimulated by the manufacture of woolen cloth). The depletion of England's own natural resources, especially its forests, made it convenient to consider establishing overseas companies to produce commodities which were becoming increasingly more difficult to produce in England: potash, timber, pitch, tar, resin, iron and copper. It was to produce these commodities that Jamestown was founded in 1607.

> The staple and certain Commodities we have are Soap-ashes, pitch, tar, dyes of sundry sorts and rich values, timber for all uses, fishing for sturgeon... making of glass and iron, and no improbable hope of richer mines.[8]

Manufactures of this sort, plus subsistence agriculture, proved to be the mainstay of the more northerly colonies and were later to establish the United States, at least in the North, as an important industrial power. From Maryland on south, however, the colonists quickly switched to tobacco-growing as their basic commercial activity. Whether agriculture or manufacturing was the principal concern of a given colony, labor, as always, was the main problem. There were plenty of Englishmen eager to settle in the New World but the price of the Atlantic passage was high. The system developed to overcome this obstacle was indentured servitude, whereby the price of passage was advanced, to be worked off, usually in five to eight years, after which the immigrant would be free to do as he might choose. Despite the high mortality rate of the early indentured servants, tens of thousands of English men and women bought passage to the New World in this fashion. The great lure of it was that once a man had worked off his debt, there was a chance to buy land at prices which were unthinkably low in comparison with those of England.

For almost one hundred years, white indentured servants were the principal source of manpower in the Anglo-Saxon colonies. Black slave manpower was a relatively late introduction. The case of Virginia would seem to be the most important and most instructive. In 1624, there were only 22 Negroes in Virginia (at a time when several thousand a year

were already pouring into Recife and Bahia). In 1640, they
had not increased to more than 150. Nine years later, when
Virginia was inhabited by 15,000 whites, there were still only
300 Negroes. It was not until 1670 that Negroes reached 5
per cent of the population.[9] After 1680 slaves began to arrive
in increasing numbers, yet it was not until the second quarter
of the eighteenth century that they exceeded 25 per cent of
the population.

In 1715 the population of all the colonies with the exception of South Carolina was overwhelmingly composed of
a white yeomanry, ex-indentured servants and wage earners.

Population of the Colonies, 1715

	WHITE	NEGRO
New Hampshire	9,500	150
Massachusetts	94,000	2,000
Rhode Island	8,500	500
Connecticut	46,000	1,500
New York	27,000	4,000
New Jersey	21,000	1,500
Pennsylvania-Delaware	43,000	2,500
Maryland	40,700	9,500
Virginia	72,000	23,000
North Carolina	7,500	3,700
South Carolina	6,250	10,500

Against a total white population of 375,000, there were less
than 60,000 slaves in all of the colonies. If we consider the
four Southern colonies — Maryland, Virginia, North Carolina and South Carolina — the ratio was still almost 3 to 1
in favor of the whites.[10]

At about the same time, the total population of Brazil
is estimated to have been 300,000, of whom only 100,000 were
of European origin.[11] In other words, the ratio of whites to
non-whites was the exact opposite of what it was in the
United States. A century later (1819) in Brazil, this ratio in
favor of non-whites had climbed even higher, for out of an
estimated total of 3,618,000 Brazilians, only 834,000 or less
than 20 per cent were white.[12] At approximately the same
time in the United States (1820), 7,866,797, or more than
80 per cent of the people, out of a total population of 9,638,453

were whites. Although the Negro population was at this time overwhelmingly concentrated in the South, Negroes at no point constituted more than 38 per cent of the population of the Southern states.[13] The high point was reached in 1840; thereafter, the proportion declined steadily until by 1940 it had fallen below 25 per cent in the South and below 10 per cent for the country as a whole.

Clearly, one of the reasons why the colonial population of Brazil shows such a preponderance of non-whites during colonial times is that a large part of the population increase resulted not from in-migration but from miscegenation and the natural increase of the European-Negroid-Amerindian crosses. Thus, in 1819, there were almost as many mestizos, free and slave, as there were whites, and by 1870, there were more "mixed bloods" than whites. This situation reversed itself toward the end of the nineteenth century after the first great wave of European immigrants had begun to flood São Paulo and the Brazilian south. According to the 1890 census, there were 6,302,198 whites, 4,638,495 mixed types and 2,097,426 Negroes.[14] This "whitening" trend has continued until the present day, when whites number about 62 per cent of the population, mixed types 27 per cent and Negroes 11 per cent.[15] These figures, of course, should be read with an understanding that many persons classed as "whites" are actually "mixed" in conformity with what has previously been said about the inherent ambiguity of racial classification in Brazil.

There is no doubt that the number of Brazilians of color who were free was always greater than the number of free Negroes in the United States, absolutely and in proportion to the number of slaves. But the disparity may not have been as great as many people believe. Thus in 1819, when there were anywhere from 1,500,000 to 2 million slaves in Brazil, there were about 585,000 free men of color (not counting Indians),[16] while in the United States in 1820, 1,538,000 slaves were matched by 233,634 free Negroes.[17] Conservatively, therefore, one might claim that in Brazil there were only about twice as many free Negroes in proportion to slaves as in the United States. This fact permits us to place the claims for a higher rate of manumission in Brazil in proper perspective and leads us directly to the most important question about the demographic patterns under consideration. The number of free people of color in nineteenth-century Brazil is not at all startling in relationship to the number of *slaves*. What is amazing from the North American point of view is the number of free people of color in relationship to the number of *whites*.

Manumission may have been somewhat more frequent in Brazil than in the United States, but not so much more frequent that one can use it with any certainty as an indication that slavery in Brazil was a milder institution than it was in the United States. It should be borne in mind that the higher ratio of free coloreds to slaves in Brazil might to some extent represent a greater eagerness on the part of Brazilian masters to rid themselves of the care and support of aged and infirm charges. Since we know nothing about the age distribution of the free Brazilian colored population in comparison with that of the United States free colored population, it is obvious that less importance than is customary should be attached to the ratio of free to slave colored in Brazil.

But the ratio of whites to free colored is indeed astonishing, especially if one admits that many of the "whites" quite probably had non-white grandparents. The central question, therefore, is, why did the Brazilian whites permit themselves to become outnumbered by free half-castes? Several factors, none of them related to alleged special features of the Portuguese national character, readily present themselves.

In the first instance, given the chronic labor shortage in sixteenth-century Portugal and the small number of people who migrated to Brazil, the white slave-owners had no choice but to create a class of free half-castes. The reason for this is not that there was a shortage of white women, nor that Portuguese men were fatally attracted to dark females. These hoary sex fantasies explain nothing, since there is no reason why the sexual exploitation of Amerindian and Negro females had necessarily to lead to a *free* class of hybrids. The most probable explanation is that the whites had no choice in the matter. They were compelled to create an intermediate free group of half-castes to stand between them and the slaves because there were certain essential economic and military functions for which slave labor was useless, and for which no whites were available.

One of these functions was that of clearing the Indians from the sugar coast; another was the capture of Indian slaves; a third was the overseeing of Negro slaves; and a fourth was the tracking down of fugitives. The half-caste nature of most of the Indian-fighters and slave-catchers is an indubitable fact of Brazilian history. Indian-Portuguese *mamelucos* were called upon to defend Bahia and other cities against the Indians, and the hordes of people who were constantly engaged in destroying the *quilombos,* including Palmares, were also half-castes.[18] There was little help from the armed forces of the Crown:

> The land owners had to defend themselves. They were obliged to organize militarily. Within each sugar plantation, in every large estate, in the solitude of every cattle ranch, under the command of the *senhor,* there lived for this reason, a small perfectly organized army.
>
> This rabble of *mestizos* ... provided the fighting corps charged with the defense of the estates. Out of them came the *morenos,* the *cafusos,* the *mulatos,* the *carijos,* the *mamelucos* ... to guarantee the safety of the master's mills, plantations, and herds.[19]

A second great interstice filled by free half-castes was the cattle industry. The sugar plantations required for the mills and for the hauling of wood and cane, one ox and one horse per slave. These animals could not be raised in the sugar zone, where they were a menace to the unfenced cane fields and where the land was too valuable to be used for pasturage. As a matter of fact, a royal decree of 1701 prohibited cattle raising within 10 leagues of the coast.[20] The cattle industry developed first in the semi-arid portions of the state of Bahia and rapidly fanned out in all directions into the interior. Open-range mounted cowboys, for obvious reasons, cannot be slaves; nor would any self-respecting Portuguese immigrant waste his time rounding up doggies in the middle of a parched wilderness. The *vaqueiros* were a motley crew:

> . . . they were recruited from among Indians and
> mestizos as well as among fugitives from the coastal
> centers: escaped criminals, fugitive slaves, adventurers
> of every type.[21]
>
> The people who bring them [the cattle] are
> whites, *mulatos·* and Negroes and also Indians. . . .[22]
>
> The foundation of cattle ranches . . . opened new
> possibilities in the interior . . . to these new *sesmarias*
> . . . there flowed the . . . free mestizo population of every
> sort.[23]

Although the Brazilian economist Celso Furtado estimates
that only 13,000 people were supported by stock raising in
its initial phases, the capacity of both the human and the
animal population to expand rapidly in response to negative
economic trends on the coast is given great emphasis.[24]

It is also at least a reasonable hypothesis that half-
castes were used to help supplement the colony's supply of
basic food crops. That there was a perennial shortage of food
in the colonial cities and on the sugar plantations is well
established. Says Freyre, about the state of alimentation during colonial times: "Bad upon the plantations and very bad
in the cities — not only bad, but scarce."[25] It is known that
in the West Indies the concentration on sugar was so great
that much of their subsistence food requirements had to be
met by imports from New England.[26] At least in times of
high sugar prices it seems probable that the Brazilian plantations suffered the same fate:

> The profitability of the sugar business was in-
> ducive to specialization, and it is not surprising . . .
> that the entrepreneurs avoided diverting production
> factors into secondary activities, at least at times when
> the prospects of the sugar market seemed favorable.
> At such times even the production of food for the
> sustenance of the slaves was anti-economic. . . .[27]

Who then were the food growers of colonial Brazil?
Who supplied Bahia, Recife and Rio with food? Although
documentary proof is lacking, it would be most surprising if
the bulk of the small farmer class did not consist of aged and
infirm manumitted slaves, and favorite Negro concubines
who with their mulatto offspring had been set up with a bit

of marginal land. There was no one to object in Brazil, if after eight years of lash-driven labor, a broken slave was set free and permitted to squat on some fringe of the plantation.

All those interstitial types of military and economic activities which in Brazil could only be initially filled by half-caste free men were performed in the United States by the Southern yeomanry. Because the influx of Africans and the appearance of mulattoes in the United States occurred only *after* a large, intermediate class of whites had already been established, there was in effect no place for the freed slave, be he mulatto or Negro, to go.

It would be wrong, however, to create the impression that the Southern yeomanry, from whence sprang the "red-necks," "crackers" and hillbillies, were capable of intimidating the lords of the Southern plantations. The brutal treatment suffered by the small white farmers as they were driven back to the hills or into the swamps and pine barrens should suffice to set the record straight. If the slave in the South came less and less frequently to be manumitted and if the freedmen were deprived of effective citizenship, and if mulattoes were forced back into the Negro group by the descent rule, it was not because of the sentimental affinity which Southern gentlemen felt for their own "kind." To be sure, there was an intense feeling of racial solidarity among the whites, but nothing could be more in error than to suppose that the racial camaraderie of planter and yeoman was merely the adumbration of some bio-psychological tendency on the part of racially similar people to stick together and hate people who are different. Race prejudice once again explains nothing; such an explanation is precisely what the planters and yeomen came to agree upon, and what the rest of America has been sold for the last 150 years. There were alternate explanations, but these the American people has never permitted itself to learn.

The most remarkable of all the phenomena connected with the "peculiar institution" in the United States is the failure of the non-slaveholding yeomanry and poor whites who constituted three-fourths of all Southerners to destroy the plantation class.[28] These whites were as surely and as permanently the victims of the slave system as were the free half-castes and Negroes and the slaves themselves. Their entire standard of living was depressed by the presence of the slaves. Artisans, farmers and mechanics all found themselves in competition with the kind of labor force it is impossible to undersell — people who work for no wages at all! In 1860, the average annual wage among the textile workers in New England was $205; in the South, it was $145. "Even in industries that employed no slaves, the threat to employ them was always there, nonetheless."[29] The relationship between the precarious condition of the Southern white yeomen and mechanics and the slave system was known and avidly discussed by many planters, reformers and abolitionists. Some of the planters were perfectly willing to see the poor whites depressed to the level of the slaves, in the conviction that the ruling oligarchy was blessed with a divine mandate to rule over the "mudsills" — "the greasy mechanics, filthy operatives, small-fisted farmers. . . ." The slaveholders, "born to command and trained to ride their saddled underlings, assumed the usual aristocratic disdain for the 'lower order' whether Negro or white. . . ."[30] A South Carolina member of the House of Representatives overtly expressed what was probably a general feeling among the planters: "If laborers ever obtain the political power of a country, it is in fact in a state of revolution, which must end in substantially transferring property to themselves . . . unless those who have it shall appeal to the sword and a standing army to protect it."[31] Another Southern spokesman did not hesitate to admit that the Southern government was based on excluding "all of the lowest and most degraded classes . . . whether slaves or free, white or black."[32] Why this opinion of them did not penetrate the minds of the majority of the poor whites, we shall see in a moment. However, there were thousands of individuals and even organized groups of Southern yeomen and mechanics who understood that they as much as the Negroes were suffering the effects of slavery. Some of them were able to put the story together with breathtaking insight:

> When a journeyman printer *underworks* the usual rates he is considered an enemy to the balance of the fraternity, and is called a *"rat."* Now the slaveholders have *ratted* us with the 180,000 slaves till

forbearance longer on our part has become criminal. They have *ratted* us till we are unable to support ourselves with the ordinary comfort of a laborer's life. They have *ratted* us out of the social circle. They have *ratted* us out of the means of making our own schools ... They have *ratted* us out of the press. They have *ratted* us out of the legislature. ... Come, if we are not worse than brutish beasts, let us but speak the word, and slavery shall die![33]

But slavery did not succumb at the hands of those who could most easily have killed it, and who, it would seem, had every reason to want it dead. Instead, the Southern yeomanry followed the planters into a war and bled themselves white in defense of the "property" which was the cause of all their sorrow. Why? Were they so loyal to the owners of the slaves because the measure of their hatred for dark skin and curly hair was so great? They fought because they were prejudiced, but it is no ordinary prejudice that leads a man to kill another over his looks.

It is not surprising that a Negro abolitionist, Frederick Douglass, an ex-slave himself, came so close to the answer, which many Americans, including scholars of high repute, cannot face:

The slaveholders, with a craftiness peculiar to themselves, by encouraging the enmity of the poor, laboring white man against the blacks, succeeded in making the said white man almost as much a slave as the black man himself. The difference between the white slave, and the black slave, is this: the latter belongs to *one* slaveholder, and the former belongs to *all* the slaveholders, collectively. The white slave has taken from him by indirection, what the black slave has taken from him, directly, and without ceremony. Both are plundered, and by the same plunderers. The slave is robbed by his master of all his earnings above what is required for his bare physical necessities; and the white man is robbed by the slave system, of the just results of his labor, because he is flung into competition with a class of laborers who work without wages. ... At present the slaveholders blind them to this competition by keeping alive their prejudices against the slaves, •s *men* — not against them *as slaves.* They appeal to their pride, often denounce emancipation, as tending to place the white working man, on an equality with negroes, and, by this means, they succeed in drawing off the minds of the poor whites from the real fact, that, by the rich slave master, they are already regarded as but a single remove from equality with the slave.[34]

This account of the origin of the Southern race mania betrays an understandable tendency to exaggerate both the diabolism of the masters and the stupidity of the poor whites. It does not suffice to account for the equally virulent anti-Negro sentiments in the North as expressed by the Northern mobs which burned Pennsylvania Hall, destroyed the abolitionist presses, burned down a Negro orphan asylum in New York, and rioted against Negroes in almost every major Northern city during the Civil War. It does not explain why the Civil War was begun ostensibly to "save the Union" and why the Emancipation Proclamation could only be sold to the country as a military measure designed to throw additional manpower against the enemy.[35] The fact is, the Southern planters held a trump. To the abolitionists who warned both the Northern and Southern lower-class farmers and laborers that slavery would eventually drag them all down together, the planters countered that slavery was the only thing that was keeping 4 million African laborers from *immediately* taking the lands, houses and jobs which white men enjoyed. The unleashing of 4 million ex-slaves on the wage market was indeed a nightmare calculated to terrify the poor whites of both regions.

The guiding principle of the slavocracy was *divide et impera.* Its basic policy followed two lines, the first of which was to convince the white laborers that they had a material interest in the preservation of the chattel system. They were constantly told that, by consigning the hard, menial and low-paid tasks to slaves, the white workers were led to constitute a labor aristocracy which held the best and most dignified jobs, and that the latter were lucrative only because they were supported by the super-profits wrung from the unpaid labor of slaves. Unless abolitionism was "met and repelled" ... the whites would have to take over the menial jobs and the emancipated slaves would be able to compete with them in every branch of industry.[36]

White laborers, both North and South, believed that emancipation was a plot of Northern capital to lower wages and enlarge its labor pool. Insistent propaganda pounded this line across; anti-slavery men were called "Midas-eared Mammonites" who wanted to bring Southern slaves into the North to "compete with and assist in reducing the wages of the white laborer."[37] First-hand experience with the use of slaves in the South and of free Negroes in the North to break strikes made this story quite believable. And indeed, minus the allegation of complicity between abolitionists and capitalists, there was more than a grain of truth in it.[38]

One more point needs to be made before the freed United States Negro and mulatto are properly located in relationship to the immense economic and political forces which were building race relations in their country as they swept the North and South toward civil war. One gains the distinct impression that fear of slave uprisings in the United States was far more pervasive than it was in Brazil, considering the relatively large number of armed whites who confronted the defenseless, brutalized and brainwashed slaves. However, this fear was not based on miscalculation of the enemy. For unlike the case in Brazil, the enemy was not merely the slave, but an organized, vocal, persistent and steadily increasing group of skilled abolitionists who from the very day this country was founded dedicated their lives to the destruction of the slave power. Although Brazil was not entirely devoid of abolitionist sentiment early in the nineteenth century, the scope and intensity of anti-slavery agitation cannot be compared with the furor in the United States. A congressional investigating committee in 1838 was told that there were 1,400 anti-slavery societies in the United States with a membership of between 112,000 and 150,000.[39] In Brazil, the lucky slave fled to a *quilombo*, where cut off from all contact with the rest of the world, the best he could hope for was that the dogs would not find him. In the United States, however, the whole North was a vast *quilombo* in which not only were there escaped slaves but free men of all colors, actively and openly campaigning to bring an end to the thralldom of the whip. The constant patrolling of Southern roads, the fierce punishments for runaways, the laws discouraging manumission, the lumping of free mulattoes with free Negroes, their harassment and persecution and the refusal to permit either of them to reside in some of the slaveholding states, were all part and parcel of the same problem. One wonders what effect it would have had in Brazil, if the larger and more powerful part of the country had been officially dedicated to the proposition that slavery ought to be abolished, and if in every major city in that region freed Negroes and mulattoes had preached and plotted the overthrow of the system. In a sense, the Civil War did not begin in 1860, but in 1776. From the moment this country came into existence the issue of Negro rights was caught in a thousand conflicting currents and counter-currents. Under these circumstances, it hardly seems reasonable to conclude that it is our "Anglo-Saxon Protestant heritage" which is at fault. Indeed there are so many more palpable things at which to point, that I hope I will be forgiven for mentioning only the few which seem to me most important.

8 / Epilogue

One of the most profound consequences of the Latin American slave plantation system was the limitation of immigration by European homesteaders to the plantation areas. In this consequence, the slave system resembled that of the highland areas. In both cases the intensive use of non-European labor prevented the development of small-scale mixed farming by European migrants. In the highlands, the land resources were consumed in support of the Indian populations and *hacienda* interests, while the growing of commercial plantation crops in the lowlands effectively precluded the transference from Europe of any substantial number of peasant families. In both cases large mestizo populations began to develop early in the colonial period; and in both cases, it was from this mestizo group that many functions of an economic and political sort better filled by free labor were met in colonial society.

Thus, the labor systems of both the Latin American highlands and lowlands, despite their striking structural differences, were similar in their effect upon the pattern of immigration and the distribution of physical types in the hierarchy of social classes. In effect, in both cases, the labor systems prevented the development early in colonial times of a white class of small-scale European farmers. The de-emphasis of class in the United States and the emphasis on race as defined by descent, and the de-emphasis of race as defined by descent and the emphasis upon class in Latin America, do not constitute accidental correlations. This emphasis upon class is a symptom of social systems in which upward mobility is extremely difficult, or has been extremely difficult historically.

In brief, it may be said that the large Negro and mulatto population in Brazil and the large mestizo population in the highlands have not come into competition with the relatively small white components over access to higher-ranking positions. They have not come into competition because there was little opportunity for any members of the lower class to move upward in the social hierarchy. Under such circumstances it is clear that no one had anything to gain in Brazil by instituting a rigid rule of racial descent; certainly, from the point of view of the landed aristocracy, it was of little significance who was a Negro and who was a white. During slavery, the only important issue was who was a slave. After slavery, the poor whites, the mulattoes and the Negroes found themselves more or less in the same boat. The inevitable product of the Latin American slave system was a society divided into two sharply differentiated classes, with the higher-ranking of the two numerically small in comparison with the lower-ranking one. The general economic stagnation which has been characteristic of lowland Latin America since the abolition of slavery, therefore, tends to reinforce the pattern of pacific relationships among the various racial groups on the lower-ranking levels of the social hierarchy. Not only were the poor whites outnumbered by the mulattoes and Negroes, but there was very little of a significant material nature to struggle over in view of the generally static condition of the economy.

This same set of factors should also be taken into account in the highland regions. As I have previously indicated, the generally low-ranking position of the mestizo groups in highland Latin America is responsible in part for the failure of many Indian villagers to make a concerted effort to remove themselves from Indian status. Here again, the generally stagnant nature of the economic system as a direct heritage of the colonial and republican labor systems is important. In a sense, in both the highland and lowland Latin American regions racial conflict of a direct and overt sort has been kept to a minimum by virtue of the fact that there has not been too much to fight over.

In the United States, however, the disproportion between white settlers and Negro slaves and the mulatto offspring of the Negro slaves has been further aggravated by
the remarkably rapid rate of economic expansion and, hence,
the rapid rate of the appearance of middle-class positions
which the whites have sought to monopolize for themselves.

The power of the colonial labor systems over the economic destiny of the areas in which they were installed is
revealed by the fact that the plantation worlds of Latin
America and of the United States, despite the many differences which I have enumerated, actually manifested certain
startling parallels. Northern Brazil, for example, developed
a plantation aristocracy with a tradition of gracious living,
lavish hospitality and a gentlemanly dedication to arts, let-
ters and oratory. Our own Southern aristocracy later came to
resemble the Brazilians in these respects. However, the heritage of slavery crippled the economic capacity of our South
as much as it has acted as a barrier against the development
of the Brazilian North.

In comparing the economic and social development of
the United States with that of Latin America, it is well to
bear in mind that as late as the 1930s our own Southern
states constituted a genuinely underdeveloped region, characterized by poverty, illiteracy, sharecropping and a short
life expectancy. The parallel between lowland South America
and the United States extends beyond the tropical and semi-
tropical areas. It is no accident that the highest per capita
income in Latin America is to be found in the triangle between Rio de Janeiro, São Paulo and Belo Horizonte in Brazil,
corresponding precisely to the area which contained a sparse
aboriginal population and which was not used to establish
slave-operated, tropical crop plantations during the colonial
period.

As in the case of our Northern states, the southern
portions of Brazil, northern Argentina and northern Chile,
lying remote both from the slave zone and from the centers
of aboriginal civilization, were best able to attract the wave
of migrants who left Europe during the nineteenth century.
These migrants added a new and vital ingredient to Latin
America's melting pot, hitherto precluded by the dominance

of the slave systems and by debt peonage. Unlike the down-trodden slaves and the apathetic Indians, the nineteenth-century European migrants were animated by hope and a spirit of enterprise. They eventually came to set up their own small farms in the European mixed-farming tradition, or they worked for wages in the expectation that they would soon be able to buy their own lands, or start their own businesses. In the last twenty years remarkable strides toward industrialization have been registered in these more fortunate parts of Latin America. So great is the rate of growth that Brazilians now speak of two Brazils, one a high-energy, mechanized society, rapidly moving toward an economy of abundance; the other a low-energy, agricultural society, which has yet to be touched by either the French or Industrial Revolutions. Between São Paulo and Bahia or Ceará, there is the gulf which exists between New York and Mississippi or Alabama.

It thus appears that the price which the underdeveloped countries or regions of Latin America have paid for relative racial tranquillity is economic stagnation. Of course, racists in the United States would prefer to place the blame for this economic stagnation upon the presence of large numbers of Africans and Indians. The terrible irony of this position should be apparent: it was the Europeans who were responsible for the introduction of the exploitative labor systems which doomed Latin America's chances for rapid economic development. It was the Europeans who were responsible for beginning the cultivation of the tropical crops which were so highly prized in Europe and from which quick wealth could be obtained, but which gave the long-range effect of creating an inert peasant mass, psychologically, educationally and technologically ill-prepared for anything but the most rudimentary forms of subsistence agriculture. The *hacienda* system, the corporate Indian villages and the slave plantations were extensive, low-energy productive systems based upon mass, unskilled labor. Literacy, individual initiative and originality were not only unnecessary but actively combated by the slave-owners, by the Church, by the *hacendados*, and by the State, in order to promote and perpetuate the docility of the labor force.

The backwardness of vast multitudes of the New World peasantry, illiterate, unskilled, cut off from the twentieth century and its brilliant technological advances, did not simply happen by itself. These millions, about whose welfare we have suddenly been obliged to concern ourselves, were trained to their role in world history by four centuries of physical and mental conditioning. They were deliberately bottled up. Now we must either pull the cork or watch the bottle explode.

NOTES

Chapter 1. Before Columbus

1. These three divisions of Latin America correspond to what Charles Wagley (1957:4-5) has called *Indo-America, Plantation America* and *Euro-America*. The equation slights three other significant areas of South America: Paraguay, the Amazon Basin and the arid northeast of Brazil. In temperate lowland Paraguay, the people are Indian or Indian-European, and most of them speak an Indian language. In other respects, however, their culture is overwhelmingly European (Service, Helen and Elman 1954). This anomaly has been attributed to special circumstances concerning the location and missionization of the Guarani Indians (Service 1955:418-19). In the Amazon Basin, the racial and cultural mixture is European and Indian. Except for a small number of tribal groups, however, the language spoken is Portuguese or Spanish. In the arid northeast, or *sertão*, the racial mixture is European-Negro-Indian in almost equal proportions. Although Portuguese is the language spoken, and although other cultural traits are predominantly European, there has also been a considerable amount of syncretism of European-African and American cultural patterns. The relationship between this area and the plantation coast is discussed in Chapter 7.

2. The concept of levels of socio-cultural integration is described in Steward 1955:43-63.

3. For Old and New World parallelisms see Steward 1955, 178-209; Wittfogel 1957; Braidwood and Willey 1962; Macgowan, Kenneth and Hester 1962.

4. More precise classifications of aboriginal New World cultures distinguish the following areas: (1) Mesoamerica, consisting of the southern two-thirds of Mexico, all of Guatemala, western Honduras, Salvador, the Pacific Coast of Nicaragua, and northwest Costa Rica (cf. Willey 1962); (2) the Intermediate Area, consisting of eastern Honduras, eastern Nicaragua, most of Costa Rica, Panama and the Andean portion of Colombia and Venezuela; (3) the Caribbean Area, consisting of the Greater and Lesser Antilles and the Orinoco Basin; (4) the Amazon Area (Rouse 1962); and (5) the Central Andes, consisting of Ecuador, Peru, Bolivia and northern Chile (cf. Collier 1962). Steward and

Faron (1959:12-13) distinguish in addition: (1) the Southern Andean Farmers and Pastoralists of Chile; and (2) the Nomadic Hunters and Gatherers of Mato Grosso, Uruguay, Paraguay and Argentina.

The term "Highland Latin America," strictly speaking, should be restricted primarily to the areas of native civilization, i.e., Mesoamerica and the Central Andes as defined above. Steward's "Circum-Caribbean" and Rouse's "Intermediate Area" may be regarded as transitional zones between these high civilizations and the simple horticulturalists and hunters of the adjacent lowlands.

5. The most puzzling case of a civilization apparently based on slash-and-burn agriculture is that of the Maya, who during the period 900 B.C.–A.D. 700 built numerous temple centers in the midst of the Peten jungle. It should be pointed out, however, that we do not have detailed accounts of how Mayan food production was carried out. Eric Wolf has suggested: "It is more than likely that the Maya, too, possessed some system of intensive cultivation, supplementary to their slash-and-burn practices, which made use of the many lakes and swamps of the Peten. Perhaps it is this which is symbolized in their ever recurrent use of the water-lily motif in art and religious representation. It is also possible that the Peten Maya imported part of their food from the highlands" (1959:78). Whatever the solution to the mystery of Mayan productivity, the Mayan lowland temple centers were abandoned and had reverted to jungle long before the arrival of the Spaniards (Sanders 1962:43).

6. B. Meggers (1954:807) states that "... slash and burn agriculture is not sufficiently productive or permanent of locale to support large concentrations of population or stable settlements." With respect to the dilemma of the Maya, she insists that the development of the Classic period "must have been introduced from elsewhere" (*Ibid.:*817). Carneiro (1961), on the basis of data from the Kuikuru of Brazil, has challenged the alleged association between slash-and-burn and the abandonment of village sites. Although he admits that slash-and-burn plots are usually abandoned after two or three years due to infestation by weeds, he claims that the Kuikuru village has had access to sufficient forest lands to permit occupation of the same settlement over at least a ninety-year period. Slash-and-burn, Carneiro argues, is per se sufficiently productive to permit a fully sedentary way of life. Unfortunately, Carneiro's productivity statistics apply to a tribe which has been using steel tools since at least 1900. More-

over, he does not appear to take into account the heavy depopula-
tion experienced by the Brazilian Indians since the beginning
of this century. A village with a stable or declining population
might very well remain at a single site for many generations,
but this does not illuminate the normal condition of population
expansion. Meggers' position has also been severely criticized by
William Coe (1957), who correctly insists that there is no archaeological evidence in support of the theory that lowland Maya
development was an emanation from the highlands. Sanders
(1962), however, has cogently reviewed the indirect evidence for
assuming the priority of highland civilizations. Especially significant is the fact that none of the lowland sites were true urban
centers. Dispersed populations continued to be characteristic of
the Maya during their classic phase in contrast to the nucleated
settlements of the Valley of Mexico, which depended upon intensive forms of agriculture for their subsistence.

7. See Steward 1948, especially the articles by Alfred
Métraux. For descriptions of surviving tropical forest peoples,
consult Wagley and Galvão 1949; Murphy 1960; Nimuendajú 1946.

8. Descriptions of Mesoamerican architectural accomplishments are to be found in Wolf 1959; M. Coe 1962; Vaillant
1944; Morley and Brainerd 1956.

9. Descriptions of Central Andean architectural accomplishments may be found in Mason 1957; Rowe 1946. Copious
bibliographies are available there.

10. Wolf 1959:94.

11. Rowe 1946:268.

12. *Ibid.* 185.

Chapter 2. Race, Culture and Manpower

1. The Spanish invaders were quite aware of the
centrality of the labor issue in their colonization program. Ferdinand, King of Spain, declared in 1509 with respect to Española:
"...the greatest need of the island at present is more Indians,
so that those who go there from these kingdoms to mine gold
may have Indians to mine it with." (Quoted in Simpson 1950:23.)
In 1511, warning against bringing Indian slaves from the New

World to Spain, Ferdinand again noted that "all the good of those parts lies in there being a number of Indians to work in the mines and plantations." (*Ibid.* 1950:27.)

2. Simpson 1960:94.

3. By 1585, Sir Francis Drake reported that not a single Indian was left alive on Española. The Indians of Puerto Rico, the Bahamas and Jamaica were also wiped out before 1600. (Rouse 1948.)

4. Quoted in Freyre 1956:178.

5. In Brazil the selling price of an Indian slave was one-fifth that of a Negro. (Diffie 1945:696.) According to Simonsen (1937:199) Indians were worth between 4,000 and 70,000 *reis* while the Negroes were worth between 50,000 and 300,000 *reis*.

6. Classic descriptions of African stratified societies are Herskovits 1938; Meek 1931; Rattray 1923; Roscoe 1911.

7. Wagley and Harris 1958:26.

8. Borah and Cook 1963.

9. Simpson 1938:11 ff.

10. Beltrán 1946:181 ff.

11. The New Laws abolished Indian slavery and severely limited the scope of the *encomienda*. See below.

12. The Jeronymite governors of Española in 1517 were eager to solve the Indian problem by importing Negro slaves (Simpson 1950:48). Las Casas himself has been accused of supporting this point of view, but it is clear that the great defender of the Indians was opposed to slavery, no matter which race was concerned (Hanke 1949:95; Zavala 1944). Nonetheless, all of Las Casas' efforts were directed toward the abolition of Indian slavery. Neither he nor the Church attacked the institution vigorously enough to prevent the Jesuits from owning a not inconsiderable share of the Negro slaves in Spanish America (Diffie 1945:473).

13. *Ibid.:*725.

14. *Ibid.:*66.

15. Kloosterboer 1960:90 ff. For a description of *repartimiento* in Peru, see Kubler 1946 and Rowe 1957; for Mexico

see Simpson 1938. Whetten 1961 provides a comparable description for Guatemala. In Peru the term *repartimiento* was also used to denote periodic allotments of goods which Crown officials obliged the Indians to buy.

16. A system very similar to the *repartimiento* is in current use in Portuguese Africa. Except for the weakened role of the Church, all the elements of the seventeenth-century situation are present. The Portuguese overseas labor code insists that all Africans are free to choose their mode of employment. Forced labor is specifically prohibited. Nonetheless, no man is permitted to remain "idle." However, the interpretation of what constitutes "idleness" is left to the government's administrators, and the latter are ill paid and remote from higher authority. In order to "civilize" the natives, the administrators must teach them the value of work. Idle "natives" can therefore be conscripted for employment on public works. It is specifically prohibited for the administration to supply such laborers to private interests, exactly as under the *repartimiento*. But the ill-paid administrators are easily subverted by the labor-hungry colonists. Every conceivable kind of "kickback" flourishes. Africans who have been caught sleeping in their houses in the middle of the night are said to be "volunteers" for employment at European enterprises. The entire fabric of laws designed to protect the "natives" turns out to be a sop to legal conscience. Most of the Africans are kept ignorant of their rights, while the unfortunate few who attempt to find remedies against temporary forced labor find themselves declared "undesirable" and are shipped off without trial to permanent forced-labor camps. (Harris 1958 and 1959; Duffy 1962; Figueiredo 1961). One would have to be fairly well out of touch with reality to suppose that native rights were any better protected in colonial Peru and Mexico. According to John Rowe (1957:162-3), "... the only incentive to take on the job of *corregidor* was the opportunity for graft which the post offered because of the wide powers that went with it ... Most *corregidores* came to their jobs with one idea, to make a fortune during the brief period of their administration. The only way they could do this was at the expense of the natives." Independently, at almost the same time, I had made the following observation about the administrators of Mozambique: "... administrators and chiefs-of-post are notoriously underpaid. ... Obviously men upon whom such extraordinary powers are conferred, do not lack opportunity for personal gain. Although there are many administrators whose personal standards are above reproach, the system invites many

others who readily succumb to its built-in temptations." (Harris 1959:10.)

17. Phelan 1958-59:191. Queen Isabella wrote as far back as 1503: "... because of the excessive liberty enjoyed by said Indians they avoid contact and community with Spaniards to such an extent that they will not work even for wages, but wander about idle...." (Simpson 1950:13.)

18. Whetten 1961.

19. Wolf 1956; 1957.

20. Wolf 1955.

Chapter 3. The Highland Heritage

1. Wolf 1955.

2. Cámara 1952:156, speaking of Mexico.

3. Rubio Orbe quoted in Núñez del Prado (1955:5).

4. Foster 1960:167-225; Carrasco (1961) minimizes the cultural heritage but recognizes important structural continuities.

5. Tax 1953.

6. Parsons 1936:12.

7. Julio de la Fuente 1949:44.

8. *Ibid.:*155.

9. *Ibid.:*148.

10. Wolf 1955. Carrasco claims that the "ladder system" has "survival value in that it holds the community together by checking the internal economic and social differentiation that tends to disrupt the community...." (1961:493).

11. Leslie 1960:74.

12. "The high *cargos* are restricted to those who have sufficient lands and whose livelihood does not depend on wage labor." (Wagley 1957:257.) "The chief *mayordomos* [i.e. *cargueros*] must be chosen from wealthy families that own or have access to town houses" (Bunzel 1952:190).

13. La Farge 1947:137.

14. "Class distinctions were marked" (Lewis 1951:51).

15. Rowe 1957:190. "Spanish colonial rule was characterized by economic exploitation and personal degradation of the natives. Both features were carried to an extreme which is difficult to credit unless one is familiar with the closely similar conditions in which the Inca of today live under the domination of the descendants of their colonial masters."

16. Juan and Ulloa 1826.

17. *Ibid.*

18. Silverman 1960:40 ff.

19. Núñez del Prado 1955:17.

20. Bunzel 1952:181.

21. Whetten 1961:66 ff.

22. Wagley 1957:275.

23. Gillin 1945.

24. Foster 1948.

25. A study of the changes which occurred in the Mexican fiesta system after the 1910-20 Revolution is badly needed.

26. Tumin 1952.

27. Ziff 1960:20.

28. Tumin 1952:189-208.

29. Núñez del Prado 1955:3.

30. Tumin 1952:117-118.

31. Harris 1964.

32. Historically, the situation was much more complex. In Mexico, for example, there was official concern with the problem of distinguishing Spanish-born whites from American-born whites; whites from both Indians and Negroes; and Negroes from Indians (see Beltrán 1946:199 ff.). Neither in the United States, nor in highland Latin America, are there only *two* racial segments to be considered. Nonetheless, the evolution of these systems has

been in the direction of a clash between two large, well defined social groups with identity in one or the other associated with marked differences in political, economic and social behavior. It is the sharpness of this division and the social consequences of belonging which need to be stressed. In local situations, there is no doubt about who is or is not an Indian, and there is no significant status which is intermediate between Indian and non-Indian. I admit, however, that this pattern may be changing in some highland countries where the emergence of an intermediate group called *cholos* is reported (cf. Fried 1959). Greater ambiguity of identity will probably follow upon the achievement of social reform everywhere in the highlands, but this is a field in which there has been little methodical inquiry.

33. Harris and Kottak 1963.

34. Beltrán (1946:175 ff.) describes how the Spanish attempted to keep track of all the permutations and combinations of the "castas" without success.

35. This is a mistake made by Ralph Beals (1955:417) and others who try to analyze the highland racial situation. The mestizos are rural, economically depressed and closer to the Indian physical type. Structurally, however, the greatest social cleavage has always been between Indians on the one hand, and mestizos and Europeans on the other.

36. Referring to Guatemala's vagrancy law of 1936, Whetten notes that the law was interpreted as applicable mainly to Indians (1961:66 ff.).

37. Núñez del Prado 1955:3.

38. Wagley and Harris 1958:81-82; Lewis 1960:289-290; Kubler 1952:65-66.

39. Cline 1953:78-79.

40. Collier and Buitrón 1949.

Chapter 4. Plantation Heritage

1. Ratekin 1954:16.

2. Wolf and Mintz 1957; Stinchcombe (1961) presents an apparently independent but remarkably parallel scheme.

3. Wagley and Harris 1955:434. The most famous description of life on the colonial *engenho* plantations is that of Gilberto Freyre (1956).

4. Freyre 1956:58 ff.

5. Wagley 1959:199.

6. Paraguay is an exception previously noted.

7. Diffie 1945.

8. The remarkable cult which developed among the Quintana Roo Maya during the nineteenth-century "War of the Castes" is a case in point. This cult combined Catholic liturgy and sacraments with a talking cross (Villa Rojas 1945:20 ff.).

9. See Métraux 1959; Bastide 1960; Pierson 1942; Ribeiro 1942.

10. Rowe 1957:185.

Chapter 5. The Brazilian Pattern

1. In some parts of the Caribbean, the large-scale introduction of indentured servants from India has produced exceptions to this generalization. Thus, in British Guiana, there is a clear-cut Negro group defined in relation to East Indians.

2. These views about genetics and paleontology are derived from L. C. Dunn (1959), Dobzhansky (1962) and Livingstone (1962).

3. Harris 1964. Hypo-descent occurs when (a) descent governs membership in one of two groups which stand to each other in a superordinate-subordinate relationship; (b) an individual who has a lineal ancestor, maternal or paternal, who is or was a member of the subordinate group, is likewise a member of the subordinate group.

4. *New York Times,* September 25, 1962.

5. The Brazilian sociologist Oracy Nogueira (1955, 1959) had previously formulated the concepts of "prejudice of mark" as distinguished from "prejudice of origin," but his em-

phasis is on types of prejudice rather than on the calculus of racial identity.

6. A full report on the result of the research in Arembepe, a small fishing village north of Salvador, Bahia, is available in Kottak 1963.

7. Pierson 1955:434.

8. Kottak 1963. It would be foolhardy to try to translate any of these terms. I am convinced that the Brazilians themselves do not agree on their meaning. Considering the totally different premises of the United States and the Brazilian terminology, it is clear that no precise equivalents in English exist.

9. Harris 1964.

10. The sources for these statements will be found in Wagley (ed.) 1952; Harris 1956; Pierson 1942; Pierson 1955.

11. Freyre 1963:9.

12. See especially Harris 1952 and 1956.

13. Studies of racial prejudice carried out in São Paulo and Rio de Janeiro indicate that prejudice under certain conditions may be greatest against *mulatos* (Bastide and Fernandes 1959:364-365; Costa Pinto 1953).

14. The problems of terminological precision could be solved here if my suggested distinction between "paragroups" and "permaclones" could be employed. There are obviously paragroups of a racial sort; but there are no bisexual and multi-generational permaclones whose actor types can be defined exclusively in terms of physiological criteria. Cf. Harris 1963b.

15. Azevedo 1956.

Chapter 6. The Myth of the Friendly Master

1. Freyre 1956:4.

2. *Ibid.:*181-182.

3. Freyre 1940.

4. Freyre 1952:39.

109

5. Harris 1958; 1959; Duffy 1962; 1959. "Colonial authorities speak of Portugal's civilizing mission, but the realities of life for the Africans in the Colonies are grim. They are subject to an abusive contract labor system.... The standard of wages is among the lowest in Africa.... Social services for Africans are either minimal or nonexistent. *And, perhaps, most important of all, Africans have become the object of a growing racial prejudice created by the rapid influx of white settlers.*" (Duffy 1961:90. Italics are mine.)

6. Estatuto Indigena, May 1954, quoted in Harris 1958:7.

7. Jack 1960:7; *Recenseamento Geral,* 1953, Província de Mocambique, p. xxxi.

8. Vilakazi 1955:313.

9. Tannenbaum 1947:121-123.

10. Degler 1960:51. This article is an attack on Handlin and Handlin's (1950) theory that the differentiation between Negro and white indentured servants developed gradually during the seventeenth century and that initially there was little specifically anti-Negro discrimination or prejudice. Degler contends that "the status of the Negro in the English colonies was worked out within a framework of discrimination; that from the outset, as far as the available evidence tells us, the Negro was treated as an inferior to the white man, servant or free" (52). Degler suffers from the illusion that early examples of discriminatory treatment of Negroes in the English Colonies are relevant to the Tannenbaum (-Freyre) explanation of Latin American race relations. Somehow or other Degler has received the impression that in Latin America there was not an equally early display of discrimination. But of course, in both cases, slavery was reserved for Negroes, Indians and half-castes. Neither English nor Iberian whites were ever enslaved in the New World; surely this is an instance of discriminatory treatment. Degler explicitly accepts the Tannenbaum (-Freyre) point of view, despite the fact that his article really amounts to a denial of the significance of ideological and psychological factors in the explanation of race relations. The early *de facto* enslavement of Negroes, even when there was no body of law sanctioning slavery, is certainly a rather negative comment on Tannenbaum's use of law as evidence of behavior (see below). To conclude that slavery "... was molded by the early colonists' discrimination against the outlander" (66) is to confirm that prejudice followed discrimination, whereas it is

essential for the Tannenbaum (-Freyre) point of view that the causality be reversed.

11. Tannenbaum 1947:42; 100.

12. *Ibid.:*vii.

13. *Ibid.:* note p. 65.

14. Barclay 1827:xi-xii.

15. *Ibid.:*10.

16. *Ibid.:*11.

17. *Ibid.*

18. Mandel 1955:99.

19. Freyre 1956:392, quoting Lopes Gomes.

20. *Ibid.:*351.

21. Ramos 1939:34-35.

22. *Ibid.:*43 ff.

23. Elkins 1959:78.

24. *Ibid.*

25. Dumond 1961:8.

26. *Ibid.:*251.

27. Tannenbaum 1947:46.

28. Ortiz 1916:303.

29. Actually, quite severe laws regulating punishment of the slaves were eventually passed by the slave states. (Cf. Stampp 1956:217-221.)

30. Ortiz 1916:303-304.

31. *Ibid.:*173.

32. *Ibid.:*303-304.

33. *Ibid.:*265.

34. *Ibid.:*267.

35. Stein 1957:135.

36. *Ibid.:*136.

37. Boxer 1962:173.

38. Boxer 1963:114.

Chapter 7. The Origin of the Descent Rule

1. Dumond 1961:5.

2. *Ibid.:*16 ff.

3. *Ibid.:*120.

4. *Ibid.:*123.

5. Compare these two observations about the effects of slavery on children in the United States and Brazil: "The whole commerce between master and slave is a perpetual exercise of the most boisterous passions, the most unremitting despotism on the one part, and degrading submissions on the other. Our children see this, and learn to imitate it.... The parent storms, the child looks on, catches the lineaments of wrath, puts on the same airs in the circle of smaller slaves, gives loose to the worst of passions, and thus nursed, educated, and daily exercised in tyranny, cannot but be stamped by it with odious peculiarities." (Thomas Jefferson, quoted in Dumond 1961:28-29.) "And what are the sons of these sluggards like?... The inhumanities and the cruelties that they practice from early years upon the wretched slaves render them all but insensible to the sufferings of their neighbors.... No sooner do we acquire intelligence than we observe, on the one hand, the lack of delicacy, shamelessness, dissoluteness, and disorderly conduct of the slaves, and on the other hand the harsh treatment, the thrashings, the blows that these unfortunates receive almost every day from our elders.... And what is the inevitable result of all this, if not to render us coarse, headstrong, and full of pride?" (Lopes Gomes, quoted in Freyre 1956:392).

6. Quoted in Diffie 1945:660.

7. Furtado 1959:21.

8. Wertenbaker 1959:15, quoting the Virginia Council in 1608.

9. *Ibid.:*124.

10. Dumond 1961:374, from the Board of Trade. Georgia, which had barely emerged from Spanish control at this time,

was very sparsely populated. However, in 1761 there were an estimated 6,100 whites to fewer than 3,570 Negroes. (Greg 1941:100-101.)

11. Furtado 1959:n.81.

12. Cardozo 1960-61:247.

13. Frazier 1949:176.

14. Cardozo and Ianni 1960:247.

15. IBGE 1961:169.

16. Cardozo 1960-61:247.

17. Frazier 1949:39 and 62.

18. Cortesão and Calmon 1956:476; Oliveira Vianna 1937:86; Diffie 1945:668-673.

19. Oliveira Vianna 1937:84.

20. Simonsen 1937:228.

21. Prado Júnior n.d.:45.

22. Simonsen 1937:237, quoting Antonil.

23. *Ibid.:*232.

24. Furtado 1963:63-71.

25. Freyre 1956:57.

26. Furtado 1963:28.

27. *Ibid.:*59.

28. "Nearly three fourths of all free Southerners had no connection with slavery through either family ties or direct ownership. The 'typical' Southerner was not only a small farmer but also a nonslaveholder." (Stampp 1956:30.)

29. *Ibid.:*426.

30. Mandel 1955:38.

31. *Ibid.:*40, quoting F. W. Pichins.

32. *Ibid.:*40, quoting Edmund Ruffin.

33. *Ibid.:*50, quoting Cassius Marcellus Clay.

34. *Ibid.:*59.

35. Lincoln regarded the Thirteenth Amendment as a military measure worth a million soldiers. Williams, L. 1961:187. Wesley (1962) views the confusion over the cause of the Civil War as part of the continuing battle for Negro rights.

36. Mandel 1955:57.

37. Dumond 1961:352, quoting Henry Field James.

38. Cf. Preyes's (1961) description of Negro textile workers.

39. *Ibid.:*258; according to McManus (1961:207), "Practically every American leader during the Revolution favored some plan of emancipation."

Reference section designed by Witt-Francis Associates and produced by Maryart Studio

Glossary

aguardiente (Sp.) raw sugar cane rum.

blanco (Sp.)
branco (Port.) "white" in color, but not necessarily by descent.

caboclo (Port.) a Brazilian racial category involving some degree of Indian admixture.

cacique (Sp.) Amerindians recognized or appointed as chiefs by Spanish authorities.

candomblé (Port.) Brazilian Afro-American religious cults.

cargo (Sp.) civic and religious responsibility associated with the fiesta system.

carguero (Sp.) one who undertakes a *cargo*.

catequil (Sp.) System of forced labor equivalent to the *repartimiento*. Also, any communal labor draft in Mexico.

chinampa (Sp.) Mexican network of dredged-up fields and canals misleadingly called "floating gardens."

cofradía (Sp.) a group responsible for organizing the *fiesta* of a particular saint.

congregación (Sp.) an artificially nucleated Indian village.

conquistador (Sp.) any 15th and 16th century Spaniard who participated in the campaigns against the Amerindians.

corregidor (Sp.) an appointed official of the Spanish Crown equivalent to modern-day colonial district officers or administrators.

corregimiento (Sp.) specifically the territory and the Indians under the control of a *corregidor;* generally, a system of Indian administration.

ejido (Sp.) a grant of land distributed to the Mexican peasantry under the 20th century agrarian reform laws; formerly, village land reserved for communal pasture.

encomendero (Sp.) the recipient of an *encomienda* through award or inheritance.

encomienda (Sp.)	specifically, the power to tax and govern a group of Indians awarded to the *conquistadores* or their heirs by the Spanish Crown; generally, a system of Indian administration.
endogamy	obedience to the obligation to marry within a group of which the self is a member.
engenho (Port.)	specifically the processing plant and processing equipment of a traditional Brazilian sugar plantation; generally, a type of sugar plantation distinguished by its relatively small-scale, family ownership.
hacendado (Sp.)	the owner of a *hacienda*.
hacienda (Sp.)	an extensive agrarian enterprise based upon a dependent labor force.
ladino (Sp.)	a non-Indian, especially in Mexico and Central America.
macumba (Port.)	Afro-Brazilian cults.
mameluco (Port.)	offspring of Indian and white, especially in colonial Brazil.
mandamiento (Sp.)	term used in Guatemala for *repartimiento* labor system.
mayordomo (Sp.)	an official in the civil-religious hierarchy, especially among the highland Indians.
mestizo	culturally speaking, a non-Indian who is putatively a biological cross between Indian and white.
milpa (Sp.)	a corn field. "To make milpa" is the equivalent of "to farm" in Mexico and Guatemala.
mita, minga (Quechua)	the Peruvian and Ecuadorean equivalents of *catequil*. Systems of forced or draft labor. *Minga* is more commonly voluntary.
mitayo (Sp.)	a labor recruit in the *mita*.
mitimae (Quechua)	under the Inca, colonists who were resettled to consolidate the empire.
(os) pobres (Port.)	literally "poor", but colloquially equivalent in Brazil to colored people.
peon (Sp.)	according to context, 1) any agricultural wage laborer; 2) a debt slave on a *hacienda*.

principales	the group of senior Indians who are the unofficial leaders of many highland communities.
quilombo (Port.)	communities of escaped slaves in Brazil.
quipu (Quechua)	Knotted strings used by Incas for record keeping.
reducción (Sp.)	same as *congregación;* artifical villages.
repartimiento (Sp.)	Crown-controlled system of labor recruitment which replaced *encomienda.* Alternately, a colonial administrative district and the periodic forced sale of goods to Indians in that district.
senhor de engenho (Port.) **senor de ingenio (Sp.)**	the master of a sugar plantation.
sertão (Port.)	the Brazilian hinterland.
shaman	a medicine man. A combination folk doctor and part-time priest.
Siete Partidas (Sp.)	thirteenth century code of laws establishing the rights and obligations of the various ranks of Spanish feudal society.
teniente político (Sp.)	low-level political appointee in Ecuador who is directly responsible for law and order in Indian villages.
usina (Port.)	specifically, a large steam-driven sugar mill. Generally, any industrial plant.
vaqueiro (Port.)	cowboy.
visitadores de idolatría (Sp.)	special inquisition organized to suppress aboriginal heresies.
vodún	voodoo. Afro-Haitian cults.

BIBLIOGRAPHY

Alden, Dauril
   1963   The Population of Brazil in the Late Eighteenth Century: A
           Preliminary Survey, *Hispanic-American Historical Review*
           43:173-205.

Azevedo, Thales de
   1956   Classes sociais e grupos de prestígio na Bahia, *Arquivos da
           Universidade da Bahia* (Faculdade de Filosofia), V.

Barclay, Alexander
   1827   *A Practical View of the Present State of Slavery in the
           West Indies.* London, Smith, Elder & Co.

Bastide, Roger
   1960   *Les Religions afro-brésiliennes.* Paris.

Bastide, Roger, and Florestan Fernandes
   1959   *Brancos e negros em São Paulo.* São Paulo, Editora Nacional.

Beals, Ralph
   1955   Indian-Mestizo-White Relations in Spanish America, in *Race
           Relations in World Perspective*, ed. Andrew W. Lind, Hono-
           lulu, University of Hawaii Press, 412-432.

Beltrán, Gonzalo Aguirre
   1946   *La población negra de México.* Mexico, Ediciones Fuente
           Cultural.

Borah, Woodrow, and Sherburne Cook
   1960   The Population of Central Mexico in 1548, *Ibero-Americana*
           43:1-115.
   1963   The Aboriginal Population of Central Mexico on the Eve
           of the Spanish Conquest, *Ibero-Americana* 45:1-155.

Boxer, Charles
   1962   *The Golden Age of Brazil.* Berkeley, University of Cali-
           fornia Press.
   1963   *Race Relations in the Portuguese Colonial Empire, 1415-
           1825.* Oxford, Clarendon Press.

Braidwood, Robert J., and Gordon R. Willey
   1962   *Courses Toward Urban Life.* Chicago, Aldine Publishing
           Company.

Bunzel, Ruth
   1952   *Chichicastenango: A Guatemalan Village.* New York, J. J.
           Augustin.

Bureau of the Census
   1909   *A Century of Population Growth.* Washington, D. C.

119

Cámara, Fernando
1952   Religious and Political Organization, in *Heritage of Conquest*, ed. Sol Tax. Glencoe, Ill., The Free Press, 142-173.

Cardozo, Fernando Henrique, and Octávio Ianni
1960   *Côr e mobilidade social em Florianópolis*. São Paulo, Companhia Editôra Nacional (Brasiliana 307).

Cardozo, Manoel
1960-61 Slavery in Brazil as Described by Americans: 1822-1888, *The Americas* 17:241-260.

Carneiro, Robert
1961   Slash-and-Burn Cultivation among the Kuikuru and Its Implications for Cultural Development in the Amazon Basin, in *The Evolution of Horticultural Systems in Native South America*, ed. Johannes Wilbert. Caracas, *Antropólogica*, Supplement 2.

Carrasco, Pedro
1961   The Civil-Religious Hierarchy in Mesoamerican Communities: Pre-Spanish Background and Colonial Development, *American Anthropologist* 63:483-497.

Cline, Howard
1953   *The United States and Mexico*. Cambridge, Harvard University press.

Coe, Michael
1962   *Mexico*. New York, Frederick A. Praeger.

Coe, William
1957   Environmental Limitations on Maya Culture: A Re-Examination, *American Anthropologist* 59:328-335.

Collier, Donald
1962   The Central Andes, in *Courses Toward Urban Life*, ed. Robert J. Braidwood and Gordon R. Willey. Chicago, Aldine Publishing Company, 165-176.

Collier, John, and Aníbal Buitrón
1949   *The Awakening Valley*. Chicago, University of Chicago Press.

Cook, S. F., and Woodrow Borah
1960   The Indian Population of Central Mexico 1531-1610, *Ibero Americana* 44:1-109.

Cortesão, Jaime, and Pedro Calmón
1956   *Brasil*. Barcelona, Salvat Editores.

Costa Pinto, L. A. da
1953   *O negro no Rio de Janeiro*. São Paulo, Editora Nacional.

Degler, Carl
1960   Slavery and the Genesis of American Race Prejudice, *Comparative Studies in Society and History* 2:49-66.

Diffie, Bailey Wallys
1945   *Latin American Civilization: Colonial Period.* Harrisburg, The Telegraph Press.

Dobzhansky, Theodosius
1962   *Mankind Evolving.* New Haven, Yale University Press.

Duffy, James
1959   *Portuguese Africa.* Cambridge, Harvard University Press.
1961   Portugal's Colonies in Africa, *Foreign Policy Bulletin* 40:89-96.
1962   *Portugal in Africa.* Cambridge, Harvard University Press.

Dumond, Dwight Lowell
1961   *Antislavery.* Ann Arbor, University of Michigan Press.

Dunn, Ballard
1866   *Brazil, the Home for Southerners: Or, a Practical Account of What the Author, and Others, Who Visited that Country, for the Same Objects, Saw and Did in that Empire.* New York.

Dunn, L. C.
1959   *Heredity and Evolution in Human Populations.* Cambridge, Harvard University Press.

Elkins, Stanley M.
1959   *Slavery: A Problem in American Institutional and Intellectual Life.* Chicago, University of Chicago Press.

Ferguson, J. Halcro
1961   *Latin America: The Balance of Race Redressed.* London, Oxford University Press.

Figueiredo, Antônio de
1961   *Portugal and the Empire: The Truth.* London, V. Gollancz.

Foster, George
1948   *Empire's Children: The People of Tzintzuntán.* Washington, D. C., Smithsonian Institution.
1960   *Culture and Conquest: America's Spanish Heritage.* Chicago, Quadrangle Books.

Frazier, E. Franklin
1949   *The Negro in the United States.* New York, Macmillan.
1955   The Negro in the United States, in *Race Relations in World Perspective,* ed. Andrew W. Lind. Honolulu, University of Hawaii Press, 339-370.

Freyre, Gilberto
1940   *O mundo que o português criou.* Rio de Janeiro, J. Olympio.
1952   *Um brasileiro em terras portuguêsas.* Lisbon, Ediçao Livros do Brasil.
1956   *The Masters and the Slaves.* New York, Alfred A. Knopf.
1963   *New World in the Tropics: The Culture of Modern Brazil.* New York, Vintage.

Fried, Jacob
1959   The Indian and Mestizaje in Peru. Paper read at the Mexico
        City meeting of the American Anthropological Association.

Fuente, Julio de la
1949   *Yalalag: una villa Zapoteca serrana.* Mexico, Museo Na-
        cional de Antropología.

Furtado, Celso
1959   *Formaçao econômica do Brasil.* Rio de Janeiro, Editôra
        Fundo de Cultura.

1963   *The Economic Growth of Brazil, A Survey From Colonial
        to Modern Times,* tr. Ricardo W. de Aguiar and Eric Charles
        Drysdale. Berkeley, University of California Press.

Gillin, John
1945   *Moche: A Peruvian Coastal Community.* Washington, D. C.,
        Smithsonian Institution.

1948   Mestizo America, in *Most of the World,* ed. Ralph Linton.
        New York, Columbia University Press, 156-211.

Greene, Evarts B., and Virginia D. Harrington
1932   *American Population Before the Federal Census of 1790.*
        New York, Columbia University Press.

Greg, Cecil
1941   *History of Agriculture in the Southern United States to
        1860,* vol. 1. New York, Peter Smith.

Handlin, Oscar, and Mary Handlin
1950   The Origins of the Southern Labor System, *William and
        Mary Quarterly* 7:199-222.

Hanke, Lewis
1949   *Bartolomé de las Casas.* Havana.

Harris, Marvin
1952   Race and Class in Minas Velhas, in *Race and Class in Rural
        Brazil,* ed. Charles Wagley. Paris, UNESCO.

1956   *Town and Country in Brazil.* New York, Columbia Uni-
        versity Press.

1958   *Portugal's African "Wards."* New York, The American
        Committee on Africa.

1959   Labour Emigration Among the Mozambique Thonga, *Africa*
        29:50-66.

1963a   *A Taxonomy of Stratified Groups.* Washington, D. C., Pan
        American Union. In press.

1963b   *The Nature of Cultural Things.* New York, Random House.

1964   Racial Identity in Brazil. In press. *Luso-Brazilian Review.*

Harris, Marvin, and Conrad Kottak
1963   The Structural Significance of Brazilian Racial Categories.
        Sociologia, 25:203-209.

Herskovits, M. J.
1938   *Dahomey, an Ancient West African Kingdom.* 2 vols. New York, J. J. Augustin.

Instituto Brasileiro de Geografia e Estatística (IBGE)
1961   *Contribuições para o estudo da demografia do Brasil.* IBGE, Consêlho Nacional de Estatística.

Jack, Homer
1960   *Angola: Repression and Revolt in Portuguese Africa.* New York, American Committee on Africa.

Johnston, Harry
1910   *The Negro in the New World.* London, Methuen & Co.

Juan y Santacillia, and Antonio de Ulloa
1826   *Noticias secretas de América.* London.

Kahl, Joseph
1957   *The American Class Structure.* New York, Rinehart Co.

King, James F.
1953   The Colored Castes and American Representation in the Cortes of Cadiz, *Hispanic-American Historical Review* 33:33-64.

Kloosterboer, W.
1960   *Involuntary Labour Since the Abolition of Slavery.* Leiden, E. J. Brill.

Kottak, Conrad
1963   Race Relations in Arembepe. Columbia-Cornell-Harvard-Illinois Summer Field Studies Program. (Mimeographed.)

Kubler, George
1946   The Quechua in the Colonial World, in *Handbook of South American Indians,* ed. Julian H. Steward. Washington, D. C., Smithsonian Institution, vol. 2, 331-410.
1952   *The Indian Caste of Peru, 1795-1940.* Washington, D. C., Smithsonian Institution.

La Farge, Oliver
1947   *Santa Eulalia.* Chicago, University of Chicago Press.

Leslie, Charles M.
1960   *Now We Are Civilized.* Detroit, Wayne State University Press.

Lewis, Oscar
1951   *Life in a Mexican Village: Tepotzlan Restudied.* Urbana, University of Illinois Press.
1960   Mexico Since Cárdenas, in Richard Adams *et al., Social Change in Latin America Today.* Council on Foreign Relations. New York, Harper & Brothers, 285-345.

Livingstone, Frank
1962   On the Non-Existence of the Human Races, *Current Anthropology* 3:279-281.

Macgowan, Kenneth, and Joseph Hester
1962   *Early Man in the New World*. Garden City, Doubleday.

McManus, Edgar J.
1961   Antislavery Legislation in New York, *The Journal of Negro History* 46:207-216.

Mandel, Bernard
1955   *Labor: Slave and Free*. New York, Associated Authors.

Marta, Percy
1933   Slavery and Abolition in Brazil. HAHR 13:151-196.

Mason, J. Alden
1957   *The Ancient Civilizations of Peru*. Baltimore, Penguin Books.

Meek, C. K.
1931   *A Sudanese Kingdom*. London, Kegan Paul.

Meggers, Betty
1954   Environmental Limitation on the Development of Culture, *American Anthropologist* 56:806-824.

Merino, Luis
1956   *Las noticias secretas de América*. Washington, D. C., Catholic University of America.

Métraux, Alfred
1948   The Guaraní; The Tupinamba, in *Handbook of South American Indians*, ed. Julian H. Steward. Washington, D. C., Smithsonian Institution, vol. 3, 69-133.
1959   *Voodoo in Haiti*. New York, Oxford University Press.

Mintz, Sidney
1958-59 Labor and Sugar in Puerto Rico and in Jamaica, *Comparative Studies in Society and History* 1:273-281.

Morley, S. G., and G. W. Brainerd
1956   *The Ancient Maya*. 3rd ed. Stanford, Stanford University Press.

Morse, Richard M.
1953   The Negro in São Paulo, Brazil, *Journal of Negro History* 38:290-306.

Murphy, Robert
1960   *Headhunters Heritage*. Berkeley, University of California Press.

Nimuendajú, Curt
1946   *The Eastern Timbira*. University of California Publications in American Archaeology and Ethnology:41.

Nina Rodrigues, Raymundo
1945   Os africanos no Brasil. São Paulo, Companhia Editôra Nacional. 3rd ed.

Nogueira, Oracy
1955   Preconceito racial de marca e preconceito racial de origem. Anais do XXXIo Congresso Internacional de Americanistas. São Paulo.
1959   Skin Color and Social Class, in Plantation Systems of the New World. Pan American Union Social Science Monographs VII. Washington, D. C.

Núñez del Prado, Oscar
1955   Aspects of Andean Native Life, Kroeber Anthropological Society Papers 12:1-21.

Oliveira Vianna, F. J.
1937   Evolución del pueblo Brasileño. Buenos Aires.

Ortiz, Fernando
1916   Los negros esclavos. Havana.

Pares, Richard
1956   Yankees and Creoles. London, Longmans, Green.

Parsons, Elsie Clews
1936   Mitla: Town of All Souls. Chicago, University of Chicago Press.

Phelan, John L.
1958-59 Free Versus Compulsory Labor: Mexico and the Philippines, 1540-1648, Comparative Studies in Society and History 1:189-201.

Phillips, Ulrich B.
1952   American Negro Slavery. New York, Peter Smith.

Pierson, Donald
1942   Negroes in Brazil. Chicago, University of Chicago Press.
1955   Race Relations in Portuguese America, in Race Relations in World Perspective, ed. Andrew W. Lind. Honolulu, University of Hawaii Press, 433-462.

Prado Júnior, Caio
n.d.   História econômica do Brasil. Editôra Brasiliense. 6th ed.

Preyes, Norris
1961   The Historian, the Slave, and the Ante-Bellum Textile Industry, Journal of Negro History 46:67-82.

Ramos, Arthur
1939   The Negro in Brazil. Washington, The Associated Publishers.

Ratekin, Mervyn
1954   The Early Sugar Industry in Española, Hispanic-American Historical Review 34:1-19.

Rattray, R. S.
1923   *The Ashanti.* Oxford, Clarendon Press.

1953   *Recenseamento geral da população em 1950: 1. População civilizada.* Lourenço Marques, Imprensa Nacional de Moçambique.

Ribeiro, René
1952   *Cultos afro-brasileiros do Recife.* Recife, Boletim do Instituto Joaquim Nabuco, Numéro Especial.
1956   *Religião e relações raciais.* Rio de Janeiro, Ministério de Educação e Cultura.

Rodrigues de Mello, Astrogildo
1946   *O trabalho forçado de indígenas nas lavouras de Nova Espanha.*

Rogatz, L. J.
1928   *The Fall of the Planter Class in the British Caribbean, 1763-1833.* New York, Century Co.

Rogoff, Natalie
1953   Recent Trends in Urban Occupational Mobility, in *Class, Status and Power,* ed. Reinhard Bendix and Seymour Lipset. Glencoe, Ill., The Free Press, 442-454.

Roscoe, J.
1911   *The Baganda.* London, Macmillan & Co.

Rouse, Irving
1948   The Arawak, in *Handbook of South American Indians,* ed. Julian Steward. BAE 143. Washington, D. C., Smithsonian Institution, vol. 4, 507-546.
1962   The Intermediate Area: Amazonia and the Caribbean Area, in *Courses Toward Urban Life,* ed. Robert J. Braidwood and Gordon R. Willey. Chicago, Aldine Publishing Company, 60-83.

Rowe, John H.
1946   Inca Culture at the Time of the Spanish Conquest, in *Handbook of South American Indians,* ed. Julian H. Steward. Washington, D. C., Smithsonian Institution, vol. 2, 183-330.
1957   The Incas Under Spanish Colonial Institutions, *Hispanic-American Historical Review* 37:155-191.

Rubio Orbe, Gonzalo
1946   *Nuestros Indios.* Quito, Universidad de Quito.

Sanders, William T.
1962   Cultural Ecology of Nuclear Mesoamerica, *American Anthropologist* 64:34-44.

Service, Elman
1955   Indian-European Relations in Latin America, *American Anthropologist* 57:411-425.

Service, Helen, and Elman Service
1954   *Tobatí, a Paraguayan Village.* Chicago, University of Chicago Press.

Silverman, Martin
1960   Community, State and Church. Mimeographed report of the
        Columbia-Cornell-Harvard Summer Field Studies Program.

Simmons, Ozzie
1955   The Criollo Outlook in the Mestizo Culture of Coastal Peru,
        American Anthropologist 57:107-117.

Simonsen, R.
1937   *História econômica do Brasil*, vol. 1. São Paulo, Companhia
        Editôra Nacional.

Simpson, Lesley B.
1938   *The Repartimiento System of Native Labor in New Spain
        and Guatemala.* Berkeley, University of California Press.
1950   *The Encomienda in New Spain.* Berkeley, University of Cali-
        fornia Press.
1960   *Many Mexicos.* Berkeley, University of California Press.

Stampp, Kenneth
1956   *The Peculiar Institution.* New York, Alfred A. Knopf.

Stein, Stanley
1957   *Vassouras.* Cambridge, Harvard University Press.

Steward, Julian H.
1948   The Circum-Caribbean Tribes, in *Handbook of South Amer-
        ican Indians.* BAE 143. Washington, D. C., Smithsonian
        Institution, vol. 4, 1-41.
1955   *Theory of Culture Change.* Urbana, University of Illinois
        Press.

Steward, J., and Louis Faron
1959   *Native Peoples of South America.* New York, McGraw-Hill
        Book Company, Inc.

Stinchcombe, Arthur
1961   Agricultural Enterprise and Rural Class Relations, *Ameri-
        can Journal of Sociology* 67:165-176.

Tannenbaum, Frank
1947   *Slave and Citizen.* New York, Alfred A. Knopf.

Tax, Sol
1953   *Penny Capitalism: A Guatemalan Indian Community.*
        Washington, D. C., Smithsonian Institute of Social Anthro-
        pology.

Tax, Sol, ed.
1952   *Heritage of Conquest.* Glencoe, Ill., The Free Press.

Thompson, Edgar
1935   Population Expansion and the Plantation System, *Ameri-
        can Journal of Sociology* 61:314-326.
1940a   Natural History of Agricultural Labor in the South, in
        American Studies in Honor of William K. Boyd, ed. D. K.
        Jackson. Durham, Duke University Press, 127-133.
1940b   The Planter in the Pattern of Race Relations in the South,
        Social Forces 19:244-252.
1943   The Climatic Theory of the Plantation, *Agricultural His-
        tory* 15:49.

Tumin, Melvin
    1952   *Caste in a Peasant Society*. Princeton, Princeton University
              Press.

United Nations
    1956   *Demographic Yearbook.*

Vaillant, George
    1944   *The Aztecs of Mexico.* New York, Doubleday.

Vilakazi, Absolom
    1955   Race Relations in South Africa, in *Race Relations in World
              Perspective*, ed. Andrew W. Lind. Honolulu, University of
              Hawaii Press.

Villa Rojas, Afonso
    1945   *The Maya of East Central Quintana Roo.* Washington,
              D. C., Carnegie Institution.

Wagley, Charles
    1957   *Santiago Chimaltenango.* Guatemala City, Seminario de
              Integración Social Guatemalteca.

    1958   On the Concept of Social Race in the Americas, *Actas del
              Congreso Internacional de Americanistas* 33. San José.

    1959   Recent Studies of Caribbean Local Societies, in *The Carib-
              bean: Natural Resources*, ed. Curtis Wilgus. Gainsville,
              University of Florida Press, 193-204.

    1960   Plantation America: A Culture Sphere, in *Caribbean
              Studies: A Symposium*, ed. Vera Rubin. Seattle, University
              of Washington Press.

Wagley, Charles, ed.
    1952   *Race and Class in Rural Brazil.* Paris, UNESCO.

Wagley, Charles, and Eduardo Galvão
    1949   *The Tenetehara Indians of Brazil.* New York, Columbia
              University Press.

Wagley, Charles, and Marvin Harris
    1955   A Typology of Latin American Subcultures, *American
              Anthropologist* 57:428-451.

    1958   *Minorities in the New World.* New York, Columbia Uni-
              versity Press.

Wertenbaker, Thomas J.
    1959   *The Planters of Colonial Virginia.* New York, Russell and
              Russell.

Wesley, Charles
    1962   The Civil War and the Negro-American, *The Journal of
              Negro History* 47:77-96.

Whetten, Nathan Laselle
    1948   *Rural Mexico.* Chicago, University of Chicago Press.
    1961   *Guatemala: The Land and the People.* New Haven, Yale
              University Press.

Wilbert, Johannes, ed.
1961   *The Evolution of Horticultural Systems in Native South America*. Caracas, *Antropológica*, Supplement 2.

Willey, Gordon R.
1962   Mesoamerica, in *Courses Toward Urban Life*, ed. Robert J. Braidwood and Gordon R. Willey. Chicago, Aldine Publishing Company, 84-105.

Williams, Eric
1945   *Capitalism and Slavery*. Chapel Hill, University of North Carolina Press.

Williams, Lorraine
1961   Northern Intellectual Reaction to the Policy of Emancipation, *The Journal of Negro History* 46:174-188.

Wittfogel, Karl
1957   *Oriental Despotism*. New Haven, Yale University Press.

Wolf, Eric
1955   Types of Latin American Peasantry: A Preliminary Discussion, *American Anthropologist* 57:452-471.
1956   Aspects of Group Relations in a Complex Society: Mexico, *American Anthropologist* 58:1065-1078.
1957   Closed Corporate Peasant Communities in Mesoamerica and Central Java, *Southwestern Journal of Anthropology* 13:1-18.
1959   *Sons of the Shaking Earth*. Chicago, University of Chicago Press.

Wolf, Eric, and Sidney Mintz
1957   Haciendas and Plantations in Middle America and the Antilles, *Social and Economic Studies, University College of West Indies* 6:380-412.

Zavala, Silvio
1944   Las Casas, esclavista?, *Cuadernos Americanos* 3:149-154. Mexico.

Ziff, David
1960   The Interaction of a Spanish Village with Indian Villages in the Sierra of Ecuador. Columbia-Cornell-Harvard-Illinois Summer Field Studies Program. (Mimeographed.)

Index